Administration in the
Small Membership Church

Other Books in the Series

Administration
in the Small
Membership
Church

JOHN H. TYSON

Abingdon Press
Nashville

ADMINISTRATION IN THE SMALL MEMBERSHIP CHURCH

Library of Congress Cataloging-in-Publication Data

Tyson, John H., 1958-
Administration in the small membership church / John H. Tyson.
p. cm.
ISBN 978-0-687-64643-2 (binding: pbk., adhesive perfect : alk. paper)
1. Church management.   2. Small churches.   I. Title.

BV652.T97 2007
254—dc22

2007022985

07 08 09 10 11 12 13 14 15 16—10 9 8 7 6 5 4 3 2 1

MANUFACTURED IN THE UNITED STATES OF AMERICA

To my father, the Reverend George
Hart Tyson Sr.

Contents

But I Hate Church Administration!

But I hate it! I hate administration!

It is a bit ironic when you think about it. Most of us spend more time doing church administration than any other single task of ministry, and yet it is the one chore many of us dislike the most. As I was preparing to write this, I called many of my colleagues in ministry to poll them. I spoke with ministers from several denominations and from many different church environments: new church plants, small, medium, and large churches, contemporary and traditional. But it was pretty much unanimous — everybody hates church administration and everybody has a lot of it to do. In fact, many of us spend about one-third of our ministry hours doing administration. Several pastors even estimate that it takes as much as 50 percent to 60 percent of their time. The general consensus was "I hate it, but I have to do it."

But I did not have to poll colleagues to learn about getting into trouble because of poor administrative leadership. During my first pastorate after divinity school, I received baptism by fire. No one complained about my incomplete knowledge of scripture, no one openly questioned my theology, and no one cared how much or how little I knew about church history. But I was not so fortunate in the area of church administration and leadership.

There was the time that I promised to be the speaker at our women's banquet on the same weekend that I had planned to take the youth skiing. I did not realize that I had a schedule conflict until I was putting together the information for the monthly newsletter. When I told our volunteer editor of my mistake and asked her advice for solving the conflicting dates, her reaction shocked me. She was absolutely furious. I mean furious! This silver-haired lady shook with rage as she informed me that she, and many others in the congregation, had been aware for two months that I had double-booked that weekend, and they had been waiting to see how long it would take me to realize it. She ranted for what seemed like ten minutes before reaching the climax of her frustration, hurling her parting epithet: "Why don't you grow up? Just grow up!"

More than twenty years later, I still remember that scene vividly. This woman had retired after an outstanding career in administrative work in the county government, and both she and her husband were leaders in county politics as well as in our church. My ineptness at basic administrative leadership indicated to her a lack of maturity or a lack of caring. But it was neither. It was a lack of training. At that time, I did not know how to keep a day planner with the kind of skill that ensured nothing slipped through the cracks. And the truth is, I was in ministry for many years and had made many administrative gaffes, before I gradually gleaned the necessary skills.

Another incident, which is lodged in my memory, happened at this same church. A prominent member placed two enormous bouquets of roses in the sanctuary in memory of her mother. This occasion was important enough to her that she told me about it (only once) three months in advance, so that I would be sure to print the tribute in the church bulletin. I remember thinking at the time "This is difficult; I have to remember this for three months!" I wrote the information down, put it in my desk drawer, and assumed I would remember to retrieve it at the right time. Unfortunately, my memory was not quite sharp enough, even at the age of 26, and I forgot. When the Sunday morning arrived and I saw the roses in the sanctuary, my stomach knotted. I went immediately to the woman, confessed my omission, and apologized. When I suggested that I could announce it verbally, she looked at me with utter disgust and said, "No. Do not mention it. Everyone knows anyway."

I had expected this woman to be disappointed, but also to be kind and forgiving. After all, I had meant to remember. My failure was not a failure to care, it was just an administrative failure to remember a detail at the right time. More accurately, it was not a failure to *feel* care; it was a failure to *deliver* care. As it turns out, since the results are the same, parishioners cannot distinguish between the two. Although ministry originates in the heart, it is not merely an inner feeling of holy love for others; ministry is the appropriate expression and delivery of holy love. The emotion of holy love is a profound virtue. But if the emotion of holy love does not administratively follow through to the delivery of care, it isn't ministry.

I remember this incident, not because my mistake was a shameful or monumental character flaw, but because this small administrative gap cost me this woman's trust, respect, and goodwill. They were never regained. Worse, she was a leader in the church, which meant that her leadership with others was no longer available to work under the umbrella of my leadership. She was not going to encourage others to trust and follow me, because her personal experience was that I could not be trusted in relatively small matters. Due to either my incompetence or my indifference, and she could not distinguish between the two, I could not be trusted to follow through on a simple bulletin announcement. She was not inclined to trust me in leadership areas where the stakes were higher.

These two stories demonstrate the need for administrative leadership at a very basic level. Learning to store information so that we can forget about it and then retrieve it at just the right time is a rudimentary skill. We don't have to be gifted to do this, we just need to have a system and believe that the pain of failure is greater than the pain of sticking with the system. Some of these basic levels of administrative ability will be defined when we discuss managing ourselves. Managing and leading is far more challenging, and some of us may want to just skim the first half of the book before digging into the later chapters. But for most of us, a review of self-management skills will be a useful brush up.

There are obviously other important gifts for ministry, besides administration and leadership, such as preaching, teaching, evangelism, and pastoring. It is probably out of desire to exercise these gifts that most of us enter ordained ministry. But no matter how beautifully we preach, no matter how soundly we teach, no matter how profoundly we care for the sorrows and joys of others, if we fail in administration and leadership, we will eventually fail in the other areas as well. Stirring preaching, inspiring teaching, and fervent caring will eventually rise or fall with our administrative abilities to structure worship planning, execute a carefully planned curriculum, and make follow-up calls after a pastoral crisis has passed. No matter how much we care, caring alone does not guarantee that we will remember to show up at the right time. Only sound administrative skills will give us the structure to deliver our heartfelt care, even on days when we are so harried that a mere mortal might have forgotten that tomorrow is the first anniversary of Miss Sadie's husband's death.

The good news is that you will never forget again if you decide to use the plan I will share with you (in chapter 2). Of course, I wish I could tell you I never make administrative mistakes anymore. The truth is, I only make them when I become so confident that I skip a few days of using the system I will share with you.

One reason many of us don't like church administration is because we may not be very good at it. That really makes a disastrous combination! We aren't very skilled at church administration and people are yelling at us when we make a mistake: "Why don't you just grow up!" (or whatever your difficult people yell at you when you botch things up). And why aren't we very good at church administration? The most obvious explanation is that we are probably not naturally gifted in the area of administration. Oswald and Kroeger suggest that only about 7 percent of clergy have the ideal personality type to be natural administrators and that ESTJs (Extravert-Sensing-Thinking-Judging types), in

Myers-Briggs parlance, are most adept at parish administration. It's not surprising then, that they further estimate approximately 7 percent of clergy have that personality type. (Roy M. Oswald and Otto Kroeger, *Personality Type and Religious Leadership* [n.p.: Alban Institute, 1988]).

Most of us are gifted in areas of ministry that are either introverted spiritual functions, such as interpreting scripture, praying, and meditating, or extroverted spiritual functions such as preaching, teaching, and counseling. But for the majority of us, our natural giftedness is probably not parish administration.

Compounding the problem of our disinclination toward administrative matters is the fact that many seminaries do not emphasize the importance of leadership and church administration. This is probably because religious academics have a touch of disdain for the "technical" aspects of parish life. Administrative concerns are brushed aside as technical skills (think of the phrase "community technical college" to grasp the disdain) that can be picked up in the parish or that are taught in business schools (again, disdain). It is generally thought that teaching seminary courses on parish administration is both unnecessary and unwise: far better to spend that course time learning about the gnostics of the second century. Well, nobody in the parish ever asked me about Gnosticism (though I tell them about it anyway) but everybody wants to know if I can administer the priorities of my local church's ministry. More to the point, my parishioners want to know if I am going to remember them on their big day, whatever that "big day" is for them. Yet, many of us graduate from seminary with the impression that church administration is neither very difficult nor terribly important. Then we may wake up one day to discover that we spend far more hours per week in administration than in any other single pastoral duty, that these skills come neither easily nor naturally, and that they may well be the single most determinative skill-set in the effectiveness of our pastoral role!

The good news is that we do not have to be naturally gifted administrators in order to fulfill that role with aplomb. These are skills we can learn, and use effectively, even if we are not gifted in this area. Like most skills, it is mostly a matter of taking time to learn some systems that work and then putting those systems in place so they happen almost automatically.

Administration, Leadership, and Spiritual Giftedness

Putting aside the discussion of personality type, which may indicate natural talent in certain areas, let's look at the question of spiritual giftedness for ministry. In 1 Corinthians 12, Romans 12, and Ephesians 4, we find the major lists of ministry gifts. Unlike personality type, these are given—not by genetics and environment—but by the Holy Spirit. As the Holy Spirit baptizes and fills us, he also equips us with gifts for building up the body of Christ. These gifts for ministry are given to all Christians, not just the ordained; when we are baptized, we are baptized into what Martin Luther liked to call the "priesthood of all believers." That means that each Christian has spiritual gifts for sharing in ministry with the body of Christ. An important part of Paul's point in both Romans 12 and 1 Corinthians 12 is that all of the gifts are necessary for the healthy functioning of the body of Christ. Since each of us has some of the gifts, and none of us has all of them, we must band together and share our mutual giftedness to create a fully functioning body.

One of the really encouraging aspects of Paul's teaching is that our spiritual gifts are given to us graciously by God to carry out the ministries to which he has called us. In addition, Paul encourages us to "earnestly desire the higher gifts" (1 Corinthians 12:31). This suggests that there is a beautiful synergy between God's call upon us for ministry, God's equipping us to do that ministry, and God's willingness to fulfill our earnest desires for ministry gifts, which we need in order to fulfill our call. I would encourage you to "earnestly desire" the spiritual gifts of administration and leadership, because it is very difficult to be an effective pastor without them.

Connections Between Leadership and Administration

It is almost impossible to talk about leadership and adminis-tration as though they were two separate concepts. They are so interconnected that the words are used interchangeably in scrip-ture, in pastoral teaching, and in the secular world. On the lower levels of administration, we may feel that it is relatively easy to distinguish administration from the functions of leadership. For example, my double booking the women's banquet and the ski trip looks like a purely administrative problem, not a leadership problem. And my failure to announce that roses were placed in the sanctuary in memory of a special person also looks like an administrative problem, not a leadership problem. Yet both these administrative snarls had important leadership connections.

I had difficulty leading this parish because I could not organize efficiently enough to win their trust and respect. I believe they respected my spirituality, and they validated my call to ministry. But they did not trust me to lead them effectively because they were never quite sure whether I would keep everything running smoothly. On the most basic level, we can't lead if we aren't pres-ent at the right time, in the right place, with the right equipment. Much of that is rudimentary administration: thinking our pur-pose through carefully, making a list of what is needed to accom-plish that purpose, ensuring that those things show up at the right time, and making sure that we are present to inspire, to encourage, and to lead. If we cannot organize on that basic level, we cannot lead, simply because we are not present and equipped to lead. In addition, people will follow only leaders they trust. If we can gain our people's trust in simple ways, by showing up pre-pared and on time, then we can move with them to a higher level of leadership. However, if they figure out that we can't lead and administrate, they may respect our spirituality but realize that we are not well-suited to lead their church as its pastor. Good admin-istration is inseparable from good leadership.

Perhaps the first place I noticed the scriptural connections between leadership and administration was in comparing different translations of 1 Corinthians 12:28 and Romans 12:8. The word Paul uses in Romans is *proistemi*. The KJV renders this as "ruling." The NIV, NRSV, NASB, and *New Century Version* translate it as "leading." The RSV translates it "giving aid."

The word in the Corinthian text is *kubernesis*, from which we get the English word "government." In fact, the KJV and *New Century Version* translate this as the gift of "governments" and being "able to govern." The NRSV translates it as "leadership," while the RSV, NASB, and NIV translate it as "administration." So the ministry gift, which is most often translated as leadership, can also be translated as administration. It is also interesting that even though *kubernesis* only appears here in the New Testament, its Greek cognate refers to piloting, steering, or guiding a ship or boat. "Taking the helm" of a church speaks to both leadership and administering functions.

If Bible translators see the notions of leadership and administration as being so closely allied that they are in many ways interchangeable, they are not alone. Theologians and pastors also tend to use the terms synonymously. For example, George Hunter chose to call one of his books *Leading and Administering a Growing Church*, because he discerned that leadership and administration are inseparable. A quick perusal of secular texts on leadership (both academic and popular) also shows that the two are inseparably linked. Leadership is often distinguished as "doing the right things" and administration as "doing things right." In general, the distinctions between leadership and administration have to do with subsets of a larger whole. That is, administration is a subcategory of leadership: the higher your level of leadership, the higher your level of administration; but leaders always administrate on the level of their leadership. For example, if you are leading by running the church office, you answer phones, keep office hours, print bulletins, and maintain correspondence. This is an exertion of leadership, although a low level of it. If you are leading on a higher level, you may simply inspire and supervise the people who do these administrative tasks. On a still higher level, you may inspire and supervise those who supervise the workers. But a leader must always check to ensure that her plans are being executed; otherwise, she is not a leader, but merely a philosopher. Leadership without effective administration is not leadership; it is philosophy. It has often been said that a leader without followers is not leading, she is just taking a walk!

My point is that the two are so closely related that they cannot long be separated. A great example of this commingling of leadership and administration is found throughout Jack Welch's book *Winning*. Welch is the legendary CEO who led General Electric to increase its value by $400 billion during his tenure, making GE the world's most valuable corporation at that time. Welch is indisputably one of the greatest business leaders of our time, so I was interested to note how fluidly he glides between the terminology of leadership and management. First, notice his title: he is Chief *Executive* Officer. That is, he is the one who ensures that the company's vision for the future is both understood (leadership) and executed (administration). If you read his book, and I recommend that you do, you will notice that he uses the words *leadership* and *management* almost interchangeably, as synonyms:

> One day, you become a *leader*.
>
> On Monday, you're doing what comes naturally, enjoying your job, running a project, talking and laughing with colleagues about life and work, and gossiping about how stupid management can be. Then on Tuesday, you *are management*. You're a *boss*.
>
> Suddenly, everything feels different—because it is different. *Leadership* requires distinct behaviors and attitudes, and for many people, they debut with the job.
>
> Before you are a leader, success is all about growing yourself.
>
> When you become a leader, success is all about growing others. (Jack Welch, *Winning* [New York: HarperBusiness, 2005], 61. Italics mine. Read his entire chapter on leadership, and notice

how many times he uses leadership and administration as absolute synonyms.)

Conclusion

Most of us instinctively understand that administration and leadership are inextricably bound. And interestingly, although many of us chafe at the thought of administration, our hearts beat a little faster and our backs get a little straighter when we think of leadership. The truth is, both leadership and administration have many levels. We begin with managing ourselves. We begin with understanding the importance of good administrative leadership, and then we ensure—through study, practice, prayer, and diligence-that whether we are gifted in that area or not, we are more than competent. Sure, it means learning to see that the church office is run smoothly, the bulletins are done flawlessly, and our information storage systems are so efficient that we retrieve information when we need it, with lightning speed, every time. It means we ensure that our buildings are clean, well equipped, and safe. It means that our financial system runs like clockwork. These are the basics, which, for people with great minds, can seem like a bit of a chore. But without them in place, and until we have mastered our "chores," our people will never trust us enough to allow us to lead in the really important areas, such as vision-casting and follow-through; and we will never have the thrill of learning to lead leaders, as they lead followers, in the execution of the vision we are casting. Suddenly, "administration" isn't plain vanilla anymore. It isn't drudgery: it is the path to genuinely significant pastoral ministry and to a growing, thriving church.

2

Managing Your Time, Appointments, and Records

No one likes to be embarrassed by forgetting important appointments, double booking, or losing important records. Yet, most of us can say these embarrassing things have happened to us. In this chapter we will find a few easy, but powerful, steps for developing a clear, comprehensive, and accurate system to manage time, appointments, and records: even if we don't have the spiritual gift of administration!

Nothing communicates the genuineness of pastoral care as eloquently as being present at the right time for surgeries, meetings, and speaking engagements, or remembering to enquire about the results of important medical appointments, job interviews, and so on. Nor does anything communicate the failure to care as eloquently as, "I'm terribly sorry. I forgot." The simple system shared below will ensure that forgetting will seldom, if ever, happen. **Warning:** You may have to read through it several times, and practice it to make it function smoothly for you. Be patient, because I promise you it is worth the effort. If you have trouble, you are welcome to contact me on my blog (www.john tyson.info), and I'll help you walk through it. So take a little break if you need to, and then settle in to master this system. Once you get it, your quality of life will improve significantly!

Your Time Management System

This system will allow you to make appointments, prioritize tasks, suspend and retrieve information, focus on projects, and recall important conversations. Once you understand how to do this, it isn't difficult at all; it is just a matter of using your system consistently. There are several tools that you can use to implement your system. You can go high-tech and use a PDA (personal digital assistant), low-tech and use a paper day planner, or retro and use a series of legal pads and loose-leaf notebooks. Use whatever tools fit your style and your budget—I like all three in combination.

The Primary Calendar: Never Double Book Again!

Most people use appointment calendars, but make two key mistakes. Using an appointment calendar the wrong way is a disaster because it leads to double booking (promising to be in two places at once) and excessive stress (caused by trying to remember too much at once). The great thing about these problems is that they are so easily avoided by following the first key step: write down *every* appointment in *one* calendar.

Write down every appointment. Most of us have had the experience of writing down only the appointments we thought we would forget, and then forgetting the ones we thought we would remember. For example, perhaps you teach a Bible study every Tuesday morning at 10:00. It is tempting to not write it into your appointment calendar, because you feel that you couldn't possibly forget. But two negative things happen when you don't write things into the calendar. One is that you must mentally file through your list of things to do each time you make an appointment, in order to avoid double booking. This is an extra hassle you don't need. You erode your peace of mind when you have to remember too many things at once. By writing down every appointment, you don't have to wonder or remember whether you have a schedule conflict. You will see the conflict instantly on your screen (or on paper) when you make the appointment. The other negative thing that happens when you don't write down every appointment is that you will occasionally forget something you thought you would remember—and bam! You are double booked. So the first key is to write down absolutely every appointment, even if it is one you think you could never forget.

The second key is to write every appointment into your primary calendar, before entering it on any other calendar. Most of us have several calendars. Perhaps there is one in your purse or wallet, one on the refrigerator at home, one on the PDA, one on the desktop computer, and one in your secretary's office. The problem arises when we make appointments using several calendars and occasionally forget to coordinate them. There is a simple solution to this problem: pick one primary calendar, and make an unbreakable rule that you will never, ever, schedule an appointment in any secondary calendar until you have scheduled it in the primary calendar.

The easiest way to ensure this is to make a point of always having your primary calendar with you. This is simple if you use a PDA or pocket calendar that will fit in your purse or pocket; it is also workable if you carry a day planner everywhere you go. If you use a pocket calendar, use one that has a separate line for every hour of the workday. Jumbling a bunch of appointments onto a tiny calendar square makes it difficult to see when you have a schedule conflict. You want a calendar that will automatically show you when a time slot is already filled. A PDA is perfect for this.

If someone wants to make an appointment with you when you do not have your primary calendar available, leave the onus on them: "I'm sorry, I would like to schedule an appointment with you, but I don't have my calendar with me. Would it be possible for you to call me this afternoon, or tomorrow, and we'll schedule a time to get together?" Additionally, you may want to have your family screen calls so that any messages for you go directly to your answering machine. That will eliminate the problem of family members forgetting to relay messages to you. In any case, remember the cardinal rule: always schedule appointments directly into your primary calendar. Make no verbal appointments, for you may not remember later to enter them into your primary calendar; and write no appointments on scraps of paper, for you may not remember to transfer them into your primary calendar when you get back to it. If you don't have your primary calendar with you, don't make an appointment.

The Daily Planning Time

It is useless to have all of your appointments carefully arranged if you miss them because you forget to check your calendar (yes, this is the voice of experience speaking). So the second component of managing your time and appointments is to set aside a few minutes at the same time each day to review your appointments and to set your priorities for the day. Some people like to do this at night before they go to bed, so that they will awake ready to jump into action. Others like to do this when they arrive at their office each day. I like to do this at home, before anyone else is awake in the morning. If I wait until I get into the office, I am too easily distracted by all the interactions there that I enjoy so much. Whatever time you choose, it is useful to do this early enough so that it occurs before you normally have any appointments scheduled. Otherwise, you may find yourself reviewing appointments at 8:00 a.m. only to realize that you just missed a prayer breakfast that was scheduled for 7:00. It is important to have your planning time at the same time each day; omit it only on days when you don't mind missing appointments, forgetting previous commitments, and processing other people's priorities instead of your own. During your daily planning time, it is a good idea to review the appointments for both the day and for the coming week. Looking at your appointments a week in advance ensures you won't forget the prayer breakfast that is scheduled earlier than your planning time. It will also help you keep the

14

larger picture in mind as you plan your time. During the daily planning time, you will also make your prioritized to do list.

The Prioritized To Do List

The prioritized to do list is a system that will enable you to do automatically the things that are most important to you, without having to schedule them. With this system, you have appointments, and you have a routine, but you don't try to schedule everything you want to accomplish in a day because schedules don't work for most people. This system does.

To make your prioritized to do list, simply open that function on your PDA, turn to today's date in your day planner, create a document on your computer, or write the date at the top of a piece of paper. Jot down all the things you would like to accomplish within the next twenty-four hours related to work, personal, and family concerns. There is no need to list appointments you have made, since they are already scheduled. Once you have written down everything you would like to accomplish, rank each thing as an A, B, or C. If something absolutely *must* get done today, write an A to the left of it. If it *should* get done today, give it a B. If it would be *nice* if it got done today, give it a C.

Now go through your A list and rank each item in order of priority. The highest priority A gets numbered 1, the item of next highest priority is numbered 2, and so on, until each A is numbered in order of priority. Then do the same with the Bs, and then with the Cs.

Here is the challenge: do your task list according to the order of priority you have established. Resolve that you will do no Bs until all the As are done, or at least in process. And remember, the Cs are usually far easier and more fun to do than the As, but they are essentially time wasters. Stay focused on the As as much as possible, because those are the things that you have predetermined are of most value. If anyone calls or comes by with a task for you, do not simply do it. Place it on your to do list and give it a priority rating. Then take care of it according to the priority you have assigned to it. This eliminates the "tyranny of the urgent" syndrome and keeps you in control of your time. (Remember, staying in control of your time and life reduces stress and burnout.)

At the end of the day, go through your list and make brief notes about your progress with each item. Each time you accomplish a task, you can draw a line through it or put a mark beside it. If you are in process with an item, but have not completed it, indicate that clearly. If you have delegated the task, note the name of the person delegated to do it. If you decide you really don't need to do an item, note that. If you decide you must forward an item to a future date, then suspend it (I'll show you how to do that in a moment) and make a note of when you are planning to readdress it. This way, nothing falls through the cracks and nothing gets forgotten.

Make sure you retain your dated lists. This is easy to do in a three-ring binder, on a pad, in a day planner, on your computer, or on a PDA. If you make the notations I mentioned above, these lists are invaluable. For example, what if you thought you had sent an important letter, but the person called and said they never received it? You could simply go back to your prioritized list for that day and see whether you noted that the letter was crossed off your list. If it was crossed off, you know you took care of it. If it was only listed as something to do, but you didn't note whether it was accomplished, delegated, or postponed to a future date, you won't really know whether you followed through. This actually happened to me last month. My bishop's secretary never received an important letter I was supposed to have sent sixteen months ago. I simply pulled out my prioritized to do list from sixteen months earlier and looked through it until I found the one that included an item which read: "write bishop." In addition, I had made a notation indicating that the letter had been written and mailed. (I also checked my correspondence file and found a copy of the letter I sent.) I felt better knowing that the mistake was not on my end; it was simply a case of lost mail.

Suspense Filing

There are two excellent ways, and one bad way, to suspend information until you want it again. The bad way (which I am all too familiar with from personal experience) is to leave the information spread out in your office, in plain view, so that you will see it every day until the time comes to use it. Unfortunately with this system, you wind up with piles of stuff everywhere, and the information becomes so obscured that you no longer see it when you need it, but rather must go sifting through the piles looking for it. Also, the pathetic disarray of your office makes you look like a complete incompetent. So much for the bad way!

The two good ways are pretty simple and will enable you to retrieve information effortlessly, just when you need it! It sounds too good to be true, but it isn't. The first way is to use your primary calendar, or your to do list. For example, suppose you receive an invitation to a luncheon scheduled six weeks from now. You think you may be out of town that day, but your plans are not firm yet, so you aren't ready to make a decision about attending. You will know in two weeks whether you are free to go to the luncheon. The solution is to put the invitation anywhere you like, out of sight. It could be in your upper right desk drawer, in your credenza, or stuffed under the cushion of your reading chair—put it anywhere. Then open your calendar or to do list (on paper or computer) and find the date two weeks from today. Make a note there: "respond to invitation in upper right desk drawer (or credenza, or under chair cushion)." Presto! It's done. You have put the information out of mind and out of sight until the very day you are ready to deal with it. Two weeks from now, when you open your calendar or your to do list during your time of daily planning, you will see your note and decide whether you can go to the luncheon. You can usually suspend information effectively just by deciding when you need to see it again, going to that date in your calendar or to do list, and making a note of where you have stored the information.

17

There is another good way, which gives you a special place for each item you want to suspend. Take twelve file folders and label them with the months of the year. That is, you'll have one for January, February, March, and so on, all the way through December. Place them in a file drawer. Take one more file, label it "next year," and place it behind December. Now take thirty-one files, and label them one through thirty-one. You will have one for each day of the month. Arrange them in your filing cabinet, behind the current month. For example, assume that today is February 28. Take the folder labeled "March" and place it in the front of the file. Now behind it, place all the files labeled 1-31. Go through your monthly file for March. It will contain all the papers and information you wanted to see again in March. Go through it, and drop each item into the file that corresponds to the day in March when you will need it.

For another example, assume that in January you receive a letter from a company that makes pictorial directories. You know that you want to do a pictorial directory this year, but not until summer. Simply decide which month you would like to see this letter again, for example, June, and file it in the June folder. On May 31, you will look through the June folder and see your letter from the pictorial directory company. Decide on which day in June you would like to deal with it, and drop it in the file for that day. If you know your directory committee will meet on June 4, you might drop it in the file labeled for the fourth day of the month. On the morning of June 4, when you check your suspense file, the letter you received months earlier is there at your fingertips, just when you wanted it. You did not have to look at it lying on your desk for months, and you didn't have to go searching for it in a stack of papers. It disappeared until the moment you wanted it.

So each morning when you get your mail, you will be able to sort it fairly easily. Some you will throw away. Some you will route immediately to other people, and some you will suspend. To suspend it, all you must decide is which month you want to see it again, and drop it in that folder. If you don't want to see it until next year, drop it into the "next year" folder. If you need it this month, just decide which day you will need it, and drop it in that folder. Sometime during the last week of each month, go through the next month's file, and drop the material into the folder on the day you want to see it again. You can always throw it away, or suspend it again for a future date if you don't need it when it comes up.

The key is that you must completely empty each suspense file on its assigned day. This ensures that you have dealt with all the material reserved for the day and also makes that date's file available to be used next month. For example, if today is the fifth of the month, when you empty the file labeled "5," the file automatically becomes available for materials to be held for the fifth of next month.

The Correspondence File

It is also helpful to keep a file labeled "Correspondence." When someone mails you a letter, staple the envelope to it (which bears return address and date mailed) and drop it into the correspondence file. When you write a letter, just make a copy and place it in the front of your file. By placing the new letters in the front, your file will always be chronological, which makes retrieval easy. This file is easy to keep and will reward you repeatedly. I have used mine three times in the past month. Once, to check on the letter that was not received by the bishop's office, another time to retrieve the address of someone I had written two years ago, and again to check on the details of a meeting a fellow minister had called.

If I receive an informational letter about a meeting I am to attend, I will usually suspend that letter for the date of the meeting, pull it from the correspondence file and take it with me to the meeting in my briefcase, leather notebook, or just in my pocket. It frequently has agenda items, names, and other pertinent information that are often useful. When you return from your meeting, drop the letter into the correspondence file.

19

This technique was useful recently when I went to an out-of-town meeting that was supposed to last all day. When I arrived, the chair greeted me cordially in the hallway, but asked why I was there. I replied that I was there for the meeting. He said, "You are not a member of this committee and cannot attend." I showed him my letter of invitation, and the matter was resolved immediately.

Project Files

Project files are used for important ongoing projects, and for people or groups with whom you meet regularly. For example, when we began the process of building an addition onto our church, I started a project file labeled "New Building." Whenever there was a meeting concerning the new building, I would place the notes or minutes into the front of the building file. This gave me a chronological record of everything we did. Later, after several subcommittees were formed, I made project files for each subcommittee.

I also use project files for meeting with key leaders. Whenever I have a conversation with them, I take notes about our conversation and place the notes in the front of the file associated with that leader. I also keep a record there of the plans we have made together, so that next time we meet I can review them and remember where we are in our process. This means I don't have to remember everything we decide, and I don't have to remember the date of the last time we met so I can look it up in the conversation log. When I have a project file for someone, the notes that would ordinarily go into the conversation log go into the project file instead.

I once had a staff member who always used a legal pad to take notes of our conversations. It was easy for him to keep up with our progress, because he kept this pad exclusively to take notes of our plans together. That was his way of doing a project file. He had about ten different legal pads in his desk, and he used each of them as a project file to track his conversations with important people. The downside is that the legal pads started looking ratty after they had been used a few months. If your project files are computerized, it looks cool, but PDAs take forever to enter information. I like to use binders, file folders, or a laptop. You can quickly enter the information without looking like a dork.

Record of Pastoral Visitation

For recording the dates and contents of pastoral visits that you make in person or by phone, you might prefer to use the address system in your PDA, which allows you to record names and addresses alphabetically and also allows you to record notes with each alphabetical entry. If you are using a paper system, you might find it helpful to get a loose-leaf binder and equip it with alphabetical tabs. Put filler paper in the binder, and each time you visit someone new, fill out a page just for them with their name, address, phone number, and directions to their house, if needed. Then on that page, record the date of your visit or call, and the salient points of the conversation. File the page alphabetically, using your tabs. Decide when you will call or visit this person again as soon as you hang up the phone or get in your car. While you are making your notes about the visit, go into your primary calendar and schedule the next visit or enter it on your prioritized to do list for the day when it ought to be done. This is the time when you will make the best decision about when they should be visited again because their circumstances are clearest to you at this moment. Having recorded the visit and scheduled the next one, you can completely forget about following up with this family until it pops up during your daily time of planning on the day you have scheduled the next visit. Now is also the time to decide whether to transfer their concern to your prayer list project file. When you visit next time, you will be able to review your notes and ask them how their left tear duct is doing after the procedure Dr. McCoy performed last Thursday. They will feel pleased that you cared enough to remember, and ask about, their particular situation.

The Daily Conversation Log

It happens to everyone. You are at your desk, working on your sermon, when the phone rings. It is Estelle, calling to tell you that her granddaughter, who lives out of state, is sick. She has some sort of unpronounceable complication of the digestive system and would like you to call sometime and have prayer with her. You write down the child's name, phone number, and other pertinent information on a scrap of paper lying on your desk, and assure Estelle that you will call. You enter the item on your to do list, and decide that it is "B-4" priority. You don't get to "B-4" on your priority list today.

The next morning, when you are making your prioritized to do list, Estelle's granddaughter becomes an "A-3." When you get into your office, you can no longer find the scrap of paper that holds all the pertinent information, and you are embarrassed to call Estelle back. You spend forty-five minutes riffling through papers before you find the notes from Estelle's call.

This does not ever have to happen to you again, and the solution is easy. All you need is a daily conversation log. You can use a loose-leaf binder, a notepad, a computer, a PDA, or a day planner. I prefer not to use my PDA for this, because it takes too long to turn it on, open the program, and enter the information one letter at a time. Until the technology improves, it is much quicker for me to use paper.

Each morning, when I come into my office, I put the date at the top of a clean sheet of paper. Whenever someone calls or comes by the office, I just make a quick record of the conversation. I write down their name, phone number if I don't already have it handy, the time the conversation begins, and any notes I want to remember. When the conversation ends, I simply note the time. This gives me a permanent record of all calls. At the end of the day, I can file the log in a binder or file folder.

Let's say that today is July 1, and one of your priorities is to talk with John Johnson from Allied Copy Machines about a new copier. At 9:03, you call John and he tells you about a great new copier he has available. It is the new XF23 model, it costs just $800 per year, and there is no required maintenance contract. As you begin the conversation, you have already turned to the daily conversation log on your desk and written: "9:03, John Johnson." As you talk with him, you write down the salient points of your conversation. The two of you make an appointment to meet on July 14 at 3:00 in your office. While you are still on the phone, you open your primary calendar and schedule the appointment with Johnson for 3:00 on July 14. Also write: "7/1" because that is the date in your conversation log that contains the notes from your original conversation. The conversation ends at 9:23, and you jot down the ending time as you hang up the phone.

Now fast-forward to July 14 at 3:00. John meets you for your appointment, and everything is going smoothly, until he mentions that the copier is going to cost $1300 per month and a maintenance contract is required. You check your conversation log and review your notes from July 1. Then you say to him: "John, we spoke on the phone on July 1 from 9:03 until 9:23. You quoted me a rate of $800 for the XF23. You also told me quite specifically that no maintenance agreement was required. I expect you to honor the terms you quoted at that time." Over the years, you will probably find that the conversation log will save you a great deal of embarrassment and a great deal of money. Frequently, people simply forget the terms they quote in a business conversation. By having somewhat detailed notes about conversations, people will view you as being more trustworthy and responsible, and they will be less likely to challenge you once they realize that you usually have detailed notes to support your position, not just vague memories.

Conclusion

You recall from chapter one that I had a real problem when I was asked several months in advance to place a memorial in the bulletin for some flowers. If I had known how to use a suspense calendar in the way I have described to you, I would have saved myself a lot of embarrassment. Using the system described in this chapter, you will never forget anything of importance again; but you *can* forget about trying to remember appointments, plans, and conversations. They are all written down in your system and will be at your fingertips the moment you need them.

3

Managing and Leading Worship Planning

Since confession is good for the soul, I may as well admit that I have had my share of "Saturday night specials." That is, I have begun the worship planning process on Saturday evening at about six, printed and folded the bulletin, and put together my sermon by midnight. There were usually extenuating circumstances, such as too many funerals during the week. But most often, it was because of deeper reasons that I usually did worship planning only a few days in advance. For one thing, I wanted to be sure that the sermon was fresh. That is, I wanted to deliver the sermon while I felt a certain inspiration and passion for its timeliness. Also, I didn't have a secretary demanding that the material be ready for her by Thursday. And finally, I didn't really know how to combine effective long-range planning with effective emotional engagement; it was hard for me to "feel led" to preach on a certain topic too far in advance. The truth is, I sometimes still did not feel led at midnight on Saturday. I don't recall ever having had a disastrously poor worship service, but I remember coming pretty close a few times and praying: "Lord, I know I should have planned better. If you will help me get through this today, I will be better prepared in the future." On one of those Sundays, my district superintendent showed up for worship unexpectedly. Of course, I am sure this has never happened to you.

There are some people who gather energy and momentum by planning ahead. And there are some who gather energy by waiting until a deadline is breathing down their neck. Some personality types are more creative working with others, while some work best alone. Each approach brings its own special strengths to the planning process, but it is useful to begin to notice which type you are, so you can work in ways that maximize your strengths and bring you energy. If you are the kind of person who likes to plan ahead for important things, such as the worship service, then you already know you are going to love this chapter. But if you are the kind of person who gathers energy from the creative excitement of last-minute preparation, I will show you how you can build in the adrenaline rush of sprinting toward a deadline as part of your planning process.

There are many components of an effective worship service, such as music, prayers, scripture, sermon, response, visuals, and the children's sermon. Sometimes there are also illustrations such as film clips or dramas. It takes time to coordinate these into a service with flow, diversity, and impact. The pastor who waits until Monday (or dare I say, Saturday?) to begin to craft the sermon and the service is locked into the fast-food version of feeding the congregation. Fast food once in a while is OK for both our families and our congregations, but a steady diet of it is dull and deadly.

The Holy Spirit and Worship

The God-breathed inspiration of the Holy Spirit is crucial to a worship experience, but it would be a mistake to think that God can only guide his prophets twenty-four hours in advance. After all, the Spirit inspired Isaiah to announce the birth and sacrificial death of Jesus Christ about eight hundred years in advance. That is a lot of time for preparing! While I don't think eight hundred years of lead time is necessary to the preparation of next Sunday's service, I think one year of Spirit-led preparation would be great!

We need the Holy Spirit to anoint each part of our process of planning and executing worship. We need the Spirit to anoint our thinking and discernment as we choose our worship themes, as we assemble the worship components, and as we gather for the feast of word and table. It is not a matter of seeking the Holy Spirit only as we prepare or only as we preach; we thirst for the Spirit's sustaining presence and empowerment for each step in the process from beginning to end.

Jesus teaches us to love God with all our heart, with all our soul, with all our strength, and with all our mind. Some of us function primarily from a rational point of view; we think out our sermon and worship preparation with rigorous logic. Some of us function primarily from a sense of heart-felt and emotional enthusiasm: we feel and intuitively sense the inspiration of the Holy Spirit as we plan and lead worship. Some of us approach worship primarily from our habits of spiritual formation for the soul. And some of us function primarily from our areas of physical strength through gifts of craftsmanship; we are really more comfortable constructing visuals—or better yet, helping build a house for Habitat for Humanity—as our most authentic act of worship. Yet each of us has all four of these faculties for planning and executing worship, and we benefit most when we use all four of them—when we allow our people to use all four as they engage in the planning and experience of worship. There are times in the planning process when our God-given rationality will work powerfully. Sometimes, the emotional impact of worship will direct us. The soul-strength of a faith-guided connection with God will always be part of our worship preparation. And there are times when our other strengths of craftsmanship, artistry, and execution will play their part.

Choosing a System

Topical Preaching

Perhaps the first thing is to choose a system, or overarching plan, for the worship year. Some ministers like to use a purely topical focus from week to week. The organizing principle is simply that they are preaching sermons on subjects, or topics, that they feel are important. They may preach on marriage one week, substance addiction the next, and salvation the week after that. The advantage to this system is that they pick topics that they feel are truly burning with relevance and concerning which they have some expertise.

A slightly more connected approach would be to preach topically using sermon series. For example, the minister might spend the spring preaching on the person and work of Christ, the summer preaching on the fatherhood of God, the fall focusing on the work of the Holy Spirit, and the winter preaching on the nature of the Church.

Some ministers preach topically using the concept of the Church year. That is, they preach on Advent and Christmas themes in December, soteriology during Lent, personal eschatology and pneumatology between Easter and Pentecost, and during the rest of the year they choose their themes freely.

Another variation on this theme of topical preaching is to help our congregations identify the core values or core competencies of Christian discipleship, and then use them as the basis for a year of preaching. Randy Frazee has done this to great effect. (See Frazee, *The Connecting Church* [Grand Rapids, MI: Zondervan, 2001]. Especially see page 246, which lists the core competencies upon which he has based his annual preaching themes.)

Expository Preaching

In expository preaching, the selection is based on the perceived importance of the scriptural text rather than the relevance of a topic. One way to approach the expository plan is by simply lining up a year's worth of scripture texts that are appropriate as an anchor for designing worship. Another method is to preach a series on a certain book of the Bible. I once preached a summer series from the book of Romans, using one chapter each evening. A method highly favored in liturgical circles is the use of the lectionary.

The lectionary is a group of preselected texts that cover the primary themes and stories of the Bible in a three-year cycle. There are many reasons that this is a great choice. One is the humility of working with a set of scriptures that the larger church has said are particularly useful and meaningful. Another reason is that the lectionary disciplines the preacher to preach from texts that may not be within the preacher's comfort zone. These are important texts that need to be shared and preached, but they may be texts the preacher has not yet mastered. Mastery of these texts can stretch the preacher in useful and edifying ways. Third, there are a tremendous number of sermon aids geared to the lectionary.

Some of these aids include subscription-based worship guides keyed to the lectionary (so we can get sermon outlines), commentaries, liturgical aids (prayers, litanies, calls to worship), dramas, musical suggestions, and children's sermons, also keyed to the lectionary. This means you can have a vast staff of specialists doing the grunt work for your worship planning, while you sit at your computer screen or at your desk and skim off the ideas that work best for you and your congregation. The lectionary system has a lot going for it. Use it to the degree that it is helpful.

So the first step in worship planning is to choose an architectural system that works for you, whether it is topical, textual, thematic, or lectionary. It is a worthwhile investment to spend some time praying about what system the Lord is leading you to use for the next year or so.

Times for Worship Planning

After you choose an architectural system for a year of worship planning, the next step is to decide on the rhythm of your planning schedules. You want to select your scripture texts, worship themes, and preliminary sermon titles for at least three months. For example, for the first Sunday in your planning, you may have decided to use the Gospel lesson as your primary focus. The

Gospel lesson is Luke's parable of the good Samaritan. You can obviously approach this parable from several angles. It can be centered around stewardship, kindness to those outside your own people group, mission to others in need, race relations, or love of neighbor. Let's say you decide to designate "love of neighbor" as the theme. You select the preliminary sermon title "Who is My Neighbor?" You are finished with your preliminary worship planning for this Sunday, because you have selected your scripture, theme, and sermon title. Now you are ready to plan the scripture, theme, and sermon title for the next service. The goal is to decide on these aspects of the service for at least the next three months.

In order to do this planning, you will need to calendar some planning time. Perhaps you want to set aside two or three full days for this. If your office is very quiet during the day, you may be able to block out two or three full days in the office for it. Or if there are a great many interruptions in your office, you will more likely want to go somewhere for a planning retreat. It is probably not a good idea to take your family on these planning retreats, because they will create their own interruptions. Perhaps it is a good idea go away to a church member's vacation home or some other quiet place where you can be alone with the Lord to discern his leading as you make your plans.

If you are the sort of preacher who needs a deadline to feel a creative burst of energy, this will work for you. You can tell your family, your staff-parish relations committees, and the person whose vacation home you are using that you are going away for two or three days in order to plan the next quarter's worship themes. By telling others you are blocking out this time for this purpose, you will have created a deadline for yourself. If you cannot borrow someone's vacation home, you could consider using some of your continuing education funds to rent a place for a few days of planning. Also, if you are an extrovert who does not work well alone, you can take some creative worship people with you (for obvious reasons, it is best not to take just one person with you, unless it is your spouse). When you come back, you will want to share the themes you settled on with your music people and the other members of your worship teams so they can work with you in selecting music, visuals, dramas, children's sermons, and liturgics that will support the worship themes for each Sunday.

When you first begin this planning program, you may want to consider doing the second major planning retreat the second month, rather than three months later, and then having a similar planning retreat each quarter thereafter. That way, you will always have at least three months of planning to share with other members of your teams. For example, you may have your first planning retreat in December. At that time, you would plan January, February, and March. Your second planning retreat would be in January, when you would plan for April, May, and June. Your third retreat would be in either March or April, when you would plan for July, August, and September. Your fourth retreat would be in June or July, when you would plan for October, November, and December. Your next retreat would be in either September or October, when you would plan for January, February, and March. With this planning schedule, you are always at least three months ahead in your planning, which gives plenty of time for your other worship planners to have input. If you can plan your scriptures, themes, and sermon titles six months or a year in advance, so much the better. That may mean you need to take more than two or three days for your planning retreats, but if you get six months or a year's worth of themes nailed down, it will be well worth it.

You may fear that if you block out a few days for worship planning each quarter, your people will feel that you are taking unnecessary time away from the parish. It has been my experience that the lay leadership is pleased and impressed that I take time to do advance worship planning. It demonstrates that worship is a priority, that the preacher is self-disciplined and well-organized, and it gives lay leadership and staff plenty of lead-time for their own planning. Just be sure that the folks in your congregation who are keyed into the leading of the Holy Spirit understand that you are going on a worship planning retreat specifically so that you can be attuned to God's leading. Reassure them that, as you start the process of preparing for worship services you will lead several months from now, you will be entering a process of listening for the Spirit's leading for each service right through the actual execution of the service. You will not allow any "script" to preempt the leading of the Holy Spirit; rather, you are beginning the process of seeking the Spirit's leadership months in advance so that God's guidance can be fully discerned, developed, and followed in each service.

After you have set aside two or three days for major worship planning each quarter, you will want to set aside about two days per month for putting other elements in place. At my current church, I set aside the first Monday and Tuesday in each month to meet with the director of worship arts. We spend all of those two eight-hour days choosing music and other supporting elements for the worship service. We brainstorm together to think of creative ways to develop the worship theme for each Sunday. It may include a children's choir piece, a drama, a film clip, or something else that is special. We may not think of something workable that is special for each service, but we greatly increase the creativity of most of the services by focusing on this for a couple of days out of each month. In a small church staffed with volunteers, you will want to meet with your volunteers at times that are convenient for them.

After you, as pastor, have set aside two or three days for major worship planning in each quarter, and one or two days for worship planning each month, you will want to set aside some time each week to develop these themes. This may involve meeting regularly with your directors of music, your children's ministry people, your drama teams, and so on. It is a good idea to go ahead and decide with these folks when you will meet each week to put these plans in place. These weekly meetings will probably be for only an hour or two. You will also want to decide what day your bulletins go to press each week. Thursday is about the latest I would recommend, because if you wait until Friday, and the secretary is sick, or the printer malfunctions, you will be hard-pressed to find a solution on Saturday. Whereas, if something goes awry on Thursday, you still have Friday—when most businesses are open—to find a solution. Again, your people will be favorably impressed with your dedication to planning ahead, rather than waiting until the last minute to get the bulletins done. Including an announcement in Sunday's bulletin that Fred Smith died on Saturday will not demonstrate that you are thorough; it will eloquently demonstrate that you wait until the last minute to do important things that should have been done in advance.

By the time you leave work on Wednesday, you should have all your bulletin information ready for the secretary when she arrives on Thursday morning. (If your church does not have a paid secretary, perhaps you can recruit a volunteer to print the bulletin.) Having someone else who expects your material to be ready for them by a certain time helps create a safeguard against allowing other important tasks to disrupt the timeliness of your worship preparation. This is a deadline that can play into the hands of people who find deadlines energizing. Many ministers like to include an outline of the sermon in the bulletin, which means they must have the sermon outlined by the time they leave the office on Wednesday (this is a terrific support for those of us who are chronic procrastinators). Although they have the outline worked out in advance, they are still free to develop the sermon with illustrations and nuances up until the moment they enter the pulpit. This gives those who need the adrenaline rush of deadlines, two deadlines to enjoy: the Wednesday afternoon deadline, and the one on Sunday morning. On the other hand, those who function best without pressure may want to prepare their entire sermon each week on Monday, Tuesday, and Wednesday mornings, so that they can simply review it as they prepare later in the week.

Creating the Funnel

Now that you have decided on themes for each service, you can funnel interesting material into them. Since you know up to a year's worth of worship themes in advance, you can capture and use material for sermon and worship illustrations as you come across it. Each movie you watch, each book you read, each magazine article you enjoy, can become illustrative material for your worship services. Allow me to issue you this challenge: when you finish reading a magazine article, make yourself review your future worship themes. Ask yourself "where might this article fit in?" Do the same with jokes, books, movies, and significant life events you experience. Get into the habit of asking how you can apply them to an upcoming worship service. Since you know your themes far in advance, you can drop this information into your planning folder as you come across it.

Working With Worship and Ministry Teams

It may be possible to plan and lead worship alone, but this would be a significant loss. First, it is not possible for one person to do everything that should be done to create a meaningful worship service. There simply is not enough time for the pastor to do everything alone. Second, it is not desirable for the pastor to do everything. Do you remember when you were a kid, and your mother let you help prepare dinner? Everything tasted better, everything was more exciting, because you had helped prepare it. Worship can be this way. When our laypeople have a hand in preparing worship, they find it more interesting and more meaningful. This is partly because of our natural inclination to view our own handiwork with special interest and favor: if Katherine created the bulletin cover, she is likely to think it is exceptionally meaningful. But it is also true that the process of planning worship helps the planner discover and internalize the meaning of the worship themes as she creatively interprets and expresses those themes in music, prayer, drama, visuals, and so on. Instead of worship being a one-way monologue where the pastor finds a dozen different ways to communicate ideas to the congregation, worship becomes a communal expression with many minds, hands, and voices expressing their own perspectives of the holy to one another and celebrating the goodness of God.

There are several teams that can be helpful for facilitating worship. Depending on the size of your congregations, you will want to choose the teams that are helpful and relevant to your situation. Here are some teams that many churches use:

Acolytes—to light and extinguish candles, and, sometimes, to assist with other parts of the service
Altar Guild—to ensure that the worship space is clean, prepared, and in good order
Music—hymns, anthems, children's choir, youth choir, bell choir, instrumentation, and so on (Few small churches have all of these musical groups, but most small churches have their own unique configuration of musical groups and leaders.)
Liturgics—to write or select prayers, litanies, calls to worship, and so on
Drama—to produce little skits that illustrate the theme of the day
Communion—to prepare the elements and the table
Sound—to mix the sound and keep the volume adjusted to the best levels, especially for contemporary worship
Ushers—to distribute bulletins, show people to their seats, assist with the movement of the congregation during Communion, and so on
Greeters—to give a warm welcome
Brainstormers—to share their spontaneous ideas for worship connections
Visuals—to create visual symbols of the worship theme
Projection—to project lyrics, filmed dramas, liturgics, announcements, illustrations
Children's sermon—to communicate the theme to children

Most of these teams are self-explanatory. But there are a few that you might like to hear more about—brainstormers, visuals, and projection. Brainstormers work like this: the pastor announces that anyone who would like to brainstorm about worship for the next quarter is invited to a brainstorming party. At the party, the pastor usually provides a full text copy of the scripture texts that will be used at three or four services in the next quarter. After reading the text with them, the pastor asks what it says to them. As they are talking, the pastor writes their ideas on a big sheet of newsprint with a magic marker. After everyone talks about this for a while, the pastor asks them to free-associate words that come into their minds in connection with the text, and also in connection with what may be happening on that Sunday (such as Memorial Day, New Member Sunday, Peace with Justice Day, and so on). Anything they say is ok, this is just brainstorming! Then the pastor writes the words they come up with on another sheet of newsprint. Finally, the pastor will draw a circle around two of the words at random, and everyone brainstorms on the connections between those two words. All of this gives a fresh perspective on the texts while working with the drama team, the visuals team, the music team, and others. Of course, in smaller churches, there may not be many people on each of these teams, or there may be a few teams that multitask.

"Visuals" is an easy concept: it is just a visual representation or symbol of the worship theme. We already do this at Christmas and Easter with special decorations such as Chrismon Trees, poinsettias, wreaths, fabric-draped crosses, and banks of lilies. Many of us also use paraments as visuals, because they change color to symbolize the seasons of the Christian year. For World Communion Sunday, the visual might simply be a globe placed on the altar, or it might be a basket of breads that are representative of many nationalities. On Pentecost, the visual might be a dramatic drape of translucent red fabric gently wafting in the "wind of the Spirit" created by a small, quiet, electric fan. On "back to school Sunday" the visual might be a book bag, lunch box, and football. One or two creative people can do a great job of tying in visuals with your worship themes—if they have enough advance time to think and plan.

Projections can be powerful. You may want to show an illustrative clip from a movie or a mini drama produced specially for worship. A great place to find these dramas for your drama teams is the Internet. If you try searching for "sermon illustrations" you will probably find a host of resources, or you are welcome to contact me on my website for current suggestions (www.john tyson.info).

It would be ideal to have different people in charge of each of these aspects of worship planning, because then you would have the widest participation possible. Just as the success of a financial campaign depends largely on giving many people a small part to play, effective worship planning works the same way. When people make a contribution, they feel ownership; that is, they are invested in the worship experience. This makes it more meaningful for them. It gives them a reason to show up on Sunday instead of sleeping late. However, in a small church, multitasking is a prevailing strategy.

My goal is to have one or two special things each Sunday: a drama, visuals, the youth choir, special instrumentalists, a fresh way to respond to the sermon, and so on. By having at least one special thing each Sunday, the service retains its comfortingly familiar form but also has an interesting dash of new flavor. Having only one or two special things on most Sundays creates emphasis and interest without overworking or burning out the worship teams. Of course, there are certain seasons, such as Lent, Easter, and Christmas, when we pull out all the stops. Let the number of your volunteers guide how often you introduce special things into the service. Perhaps in a small church an addition to the service once or twice each month would be a realistic goal.

If your congregation is large enough, it is useful to designate a leader for each group you use, and to encourage the leader to draw others into the group. It is good to plan to meet with this group on a regular, predetermined, calendared basis—perhaps quarterly—to share plans for the months ahead. By having your worship themes identified no less than three months in advance, you can share these with your leaders and assist them in selecting music, visuals, dramas, and so on, that connect with your theme. By limiting your special things to only one or two each Sunday, or each month, you will have time to give the necessary oversight and leadership to each group leader.

Each group leader should probably be on your worship committee or worship team. That is, your worship team would probably consist of a chair and the leaders of each team (acolytes, altar guild, Communion, drama, music, and so on). The pastor and the chair would work together to guide the team. In churches where the same ten or twenty people do everything, why not consider working the worship planning into meeting times that are already set up, so that existing teams or committees can multi-task? But don't overlook the possibility of drawing in new or inactive people who would enjoy using their creative energies in worship.

Conclusion

By selecting your lections and themes in advance, you can use the leverage of time and other people to make your worship more powerful. You will have the time to gather resources for worship far in advance and you will demonstrate to your people that you are proactive, well-organized, and interested in their contributions to worship. All these things will enhance your worship leadership and your ministry to the congregation.

4

Mapping the Congregation's Vision for Ministry

The Role of the Pastor

I magine being on vacation in New York with your family. Finding your way to several tourist attractions, you feel a bit lost, so you pull out a map and start trying to navigate with it. But instead of going straight to your destinations, you wind up even more confused. You notice that some of the street names on the map correspond with those on the ground, but the intersections and connections are completely wrong. As the day progresses, you see some great sights, enjoy some good food, and do some shopping as you wander the city; but you are frustrated because the map is confusing. Further, you are not finding your way to the sights and restaurants you had planned to enjoy. Finally, you realize that the map you have is for Chicago, not New York! Having the *right* map for your specific destination, not just *a* map, is crucial to finding your way.

Managing and leading church members and staff can be among the greatest pleasures and challenges of ministry. We are called to lead and manage our people as they seek to understand and fulfill God's vision for the body of Christ. Before we can lead laypeople and staff to live into God's preferred future for our local church, we must have a clear road map for where we are going, and how it will look, feel, sound, taste, and smell when we get there. The sharper our perception of where we are going, and the clearer our road map for getting there, the more effective our journey will be. However, when we are not sure exactly where we are going, or how to get there, our journey can feel frustrating and meaningless.

Not having a clear vision of God's preferred future for our congregation is a lot like going to a travel agent and saying, "I'd like to go somewhere nice." Before the agent can book us on a great trip, she will need to help us decide exactly what we mean by "somewhere nice." Are we talking about Yosemite or Paris? If it is Yosemite, are we talking about camping or staying in the lodge? There are a lot of nice destinations, but we have to decide our preferred destination. In the same way, there are a lot of great churches with great missions. There are churches that worship God in dignity and grandeur, while others praise him with the tuneful twang of electric guitars. There are churches that focus on the unchurched (such as Willow Creek), while others focus on ministry to a particular demographic group (such as Saddleback). There are churches that find their mission in ministering with great excellence to children, and there are those that hit their stride by being genuinely transformative in ministry to the homeless.

Before we can be truly effective in leading our people to live into God's preferred future, we have to help them discern and articulate God's vision for their future as a congregation. When we all understand clearly where we are headed, then we can give leadership to a process of mapping out a long-range plan to lead the congregation toward that destination. Once the destination and the road map are clear, we can give more effective leadership to the paid and volunteer leaders in the congregation who are fulfilling their various roles as we make the journey.

The task for us, as pastors, is to give leadership to the process of mapping out our local church's journey. What is our church's vision for the future? This is our destination. What are our church's core values? These are the interstate highways to our destination. What are our church's long-term goals? These are the roads that bring us even closer to our destination. What are our church's short-term goals? These are the city streets that will take us to the doorstep of our destination.

Listening and the Status Quo

As we think about the important process of developing vision, core values, long-term goals, and short-term goals for a congregation, we also must deal with the need to keep things running smoothly in the meantime. So perhaps the first question to discuss is maintaining the status quo. When we come to a parish, there are problems, programs, policies, and traditions already in place. It is tempting to solve some of the problems quickly, in order to score a quick victory and prove that we are effective leaders. However, we may be wise to maintain the status quo gently until we have time to assess things thoroughly. If there really were a quick and efficient solution to a problem—if it were really that easy to solve—it might have been solved before we arrived. Certainly this is not always true, but it is worth considering before being quick to offer a solution. Give a preponderance of the leadership a chance to want you to offer a solution before you tender it. Better yet, once you have worked out a solution, cause them to discover it. If they don't discern your idea as a solution, it probably isn't.

It is a good idea to keep everything going as it was before you arrived, until *you* are sure that the *leaders* are sure that *you have heard the leaders* tell you why things are as they are, and what *they* view as potential alternatives. Even if you do not think of yourself as new in a parish, it is likely that the leaders who have been in a church for thirty years or more view you as both new and transient. The truth is, there are a thousand nuances of relationships that you will never piece together in your parish, and there are many reasons things are as they are—buried far beneath the surface of our short itineration. Go slowly, tread lightly, and let decisions be made by the appropriate administrative bodies after plenty of discussion.

Decisions that the pastor makes unilaterally—or that the pastor imposes upon a committee—almost always create far more difficulties than they solve for the pastor. Newton's third law of motion says that for every action, there is an equal and opposite reaction. I have noticed that this is also true of human relationships. If the pastor pushes hard for a certain result, there will be those who push back with equal fervor. The stronger the push from the pastor, the stronger will be the reaction from some of the leaders. It is wise, therefore, always to offer an escape valve for excess pressure when we push in a certain direction.

Ideas for change in the parish are better sown as seeds than transplanted as seedlings. If the pastor can learn patiently to sow new ideas like seed among the laity and tend them carefully, many of those ideas will sprout, grow, and bear fruit. It is likely the ones that do not germinate are in an inhospitable climate; transplants of the same species probably would not survive, either, so it might be better to let the idea drop quietly.

Try hard to say little and listen much in meetings. Talk with people one on one and let them negotiate the changes in the administrative meetings. Realize that when your people shy away from making certain decisions in meetings, it is because they see obstacles that may be invisible to you. Heed them carefully. There are exceptional times when the pastor must take a bold and prophetic stand, but these occasions are probably less frequent than we think; pain and hindsight are good tutors for discerning the difference.

The Plan

The first step of the plan I will suggest is that you have a series of listening sessions that will put you in touch with what your people are thinking and will also help them hear what others are thinking. Then you will take the next step by helping them for-

mulate a list of their core values and devise a process for estab-
lishing their long-range and mid-range plans. It would be a good
idea to become familiar with this process and then share it with
some of your key leaders.

You might want to enlist the help of two or three of your major
leaders, such as staff parish chair, finance chair, church council
chair, lay leader, or other leaders who have influence. They will
assist you with each of the following tasks: obtaining the approval
of your administrative body for the listening sessions and long-
range planning committee, drawing up the invitation lists, helping determine your groupings, helping draw up your list of
questions, attending the small group meetings, and working with
you to draw conclusions as a result of the meetings.

You will want to share the overall plan with these key leaders
individually. After you and each key leader understand one
another thoroughly, you will bring them together in a group to
articulate the overall plan before it is shared with your governing
body. The rough outline of the plan is that you will invite everyone in the church to listening sessions. These will be small group
meetings where you will lead a discussion on the core values of
the church. You will also seek to ascertain what members like
best about the worship, programming, staff, and building, and
what improvements they would most like to see. This information will lay the groundwork for the long-range planning team,
which will be divided into four sub-teams: worship, programming, staff, and building. Once the long-range goals are established, the mid-range goals can be established. As you read this
chapter, you will see the details of this simple and effective plan.
You may even want to share this chapter with your key leaders.

Listening Sessions

After you and three or four of your leaders agree on the process
for casting a vision for the congregation's future and for estab-
lishing a long-range plan to get there, you will need to present

this package of ideas to the church's governing body and get their approval.

Once this is done, the first step in the process of casting vision for the congregation's future is to have a series of small group listening sessions. Whether you have been in a parish for five minutes or five years, it is always attractive when the pastor wants to listen. This is one of the few things a pastor can do that might meet with pleasure and approval from everyone. There is seldom any backlash from listening; only positive energy is created. Listening is a guaranteed win.

The goal of the listening sessions is to get the congregation to meet with you in small groups to share with one another—and with you—their vision of the congregation's past, present, and future. The greatest challenge is to decide how you want to form the small groups. You should resist the temptation to work with already established small groups for this project. It might be tempting to use small groups that are already formed, such as Sunday school classes, Bible studies, and home groups. A positive side to this idea is that it is easier to get the people together, because they have already grouped themselves. But there are several negative aspects. The first is that since the groups are already formed, people who are not active in one of the groups probably will not attend the listening session and may feel excluded. This will result in a smaller pool of respondents and will also cause some people to feel that you are not interested in them because they don't go to small group meetings. Also, people already know the active members of their small groups well. They will not become acquainted with others in the congregation by meeting in the same groups they usually meet with. Finally, if there is any antagonism between small groups, our listening sessions could become a sort of tug-of-war between the groups, with the pastor stuck in the middle as referee.

The likelihood of a tug-of-war between age groups is a good reason to avoid grouping people by age. For example, the young adult group could use this an opportunity to advance their "contemporary worship music" offensive. The older group might launch their "traditional worship" offensive. If the pastor were the only common denominator between these groups, it would place the pastor, by definition, in the middle. Placing yourself between powerful groups is a good way to get crushed. It might be useful for people of all ages to hear one another's perspectives. This way, you do not become the negotiator between age groups: they do their own negotiating.

It is a good idea to create new, intergenerational groupings of people for the purpose of the listening sessions. Get two or three influential people who know the congregation well to create the invitation list. It includes everyone on the church roll who lives locally, their families, and participants in the church who are active but are not members. The goal here is to throw your net as wide as possible, so that everyone feels included. Certainly, you want youth to attend. A decision needs to be made as to how children will be included in the listening sessions. If provisions are not made for them, then it is almost certain that both parents will not attend and will feel overlooked. It might be a good idea either to include children in the event or to provide a nursery for them at the church. If children are included, and if the event is held in a home, perhaps they could watch a movie during the meeting.

You want to divide the invitation list into groups of a manageable size. Perhaps the best way to do it is by geography or neighborhood. That is, you could get two or three people who know the membership well to group the people by neighborhood, inviting thirty or forty people who live closest together to come to the listening session. I favor this method, because even in small congregations, people have "their" side of town. It also allows the congregational leaders, who will be drawing up the lists, to have input. This is valuable in a couple of ways: it facilitates buy-in by lay leadership, and these leaders can structure the lists so that people who need to be grouped together (for reasons you may not be aware of, but that they will know instinctively) will be grouped together. If you plan on half of the active members coming, and none of the inactive members coming, you will get a pretty good estimate of how many to expect at your meetings. A few of the inactives will probably come, but your response from actives will probably be a little less than half. Of course, you know your individual situation best, so use your own estimate. In any case, it would be ideal to have between eight and sixteen people attending in each group. I have found that usually about one-fourth of the people invited attend, if the invitation list is representative of the entire congregation, including inactive people. So if you want about ten people at your session, it wouldn't hurt to invite forty, provided they weren't the forty most active people in the congregation.

Regardless of the way your groups are formed, it would be helpful if you could get two or three of your major leaders to attend each one. That way your major leaders would hear many voices, and the pastor would not be the only person to have heard everything. Again, this avoids making yourself the lone fulcrum. You share that power and that risk with others.

Once you have drawn up the invitation list and you know the number of groups you will be having, you can decide when and where you would like to have the meetings: at the church or in homes. If you want them in homes—which has an undeniably special quality—then your group will need to recruit hosts and line up the dates.

Next, you need to send out invitations. Tell the people the purpose, date, time, and place for the session to which they are invited. Also include in the invitation an easy way for people to change groups in case the date is not convenient for them (or in case they don't like the group they are in). Finally, include a list of the activities and questions you will be covering, so they can begin to contemplate their answers. It will save a lot of time in the meeting and help your people know what is going to happen if you send a copy of these questions, core values, and priorities in their invitation letter. You can ask them to do their ranking and prioritizing ahead of time so that when you get to the small group meeting it will flow faster. You might also put the questions in the newsletter, along with an article on why you want to have these listening sessions. In your newsletter article, you might outline the process for the long-range planning. You might also include a general invitation to anyone not identified, but who might be interested in attending, to inquire at the church office about a group.

Drawing Up Our List of Activities and Questions

Below are three activities you can use to elicit information from those who attend your listening sessions. Activity three is probably the most useful, but you can adapt these to work best in your situation. The length of time these exercises take will vary depending on how many, and how voluble, the participants are.

Activity 1: Core Values (30 minutes)

Here is a list of core values that has been meaningful to many churches. Ask your people what they might add to or subtract from it. (We got this list from Randy Frazee, *The Connecting Church*, [Grand Rapids, MI: Zondervan, 2001], pp. 77-79. Randy is now at Willow Creek.) Your people may have questions about some of the core values listed here, and this would be a good time to give a brief explanation. Using this information, you can help your congregation develop a list of core values. You may want to adapt this list to your own liking before you use it:

What We Believe (beliefs): trinity, salvation by grace, authority of the Bible, personal God, identity in Christ, church, humanity, compassion, eternity, and stewardship.

What We Are (virtues): joy, peace, faith, self-control, love, patience, kindness/goodness, gentleness, humility, hope.

What We Do (practices): worship, prayer, Bible study, single-mindedness, biblical community, spiritual gifts, giving away our time, giving away our money, giving away our faith, giving away our life.

Activity 2: List of Priorities (30 minutes)

Give people a list of things churches do. Ask them to rank them in order of priority. In some sense this is a false ranking, because we do not have to choose between caring for children and caring for the elderly. We can do both. But it is not likely that we give equal emphasis and equal resources to all our ministry priorities. With whom does the staff spend more time? What line items in the budget get greater funding? These are realities of prioritization. Wouldn't it be better to discuss our priorities so we can be intentional about implementing them? Your list might look something like this:

Making disciples
Worshiping God
Caring for the poor and needy in our congregation
Caring for the poor and needy in our community
Caring for the poor and needy in our world
Preserving and maintaining our building
Supporting our denomination's programs and objectives
Children
Youth
Families
Middle adults
Older adults
Teaching stewardship and giving
Prayer
Bible study
Preserving our past
Creating a future that is relevant to our community's needs
Helping irreligious people know Jesus Christ as Lord and
    Savior
Sunday school
Small groups
Music
Building a new facility
Paying off a mortgage
Reaching out across cultural and interracial lines

Activity 3: Personal Stories (60 minutes)
Plan on each person present taking about three minutes to answer each question. The goal is to hear about their individual views of the past, present, and future of your church. The follow-

ing are some good questions. Let each person answer one of the questions in each section: past, present, and future. Let everyone share their answer about the past, before moving on to the present and future.

Past (15 minutes)
1. When you think back over your past years at this church, what things seem most significant to you about its worship, programming, staff, and buildings?
2. What brought you to this church?
3. Was there a time that seems like a "golden age" at this church? What made it this way?

Present (15 minutes)
4. What do you like best about this church's worship?
5. What do you like best about this church's programming?
6. What do you like best about this church's staffing!
7. What do you like best about this church's buildings?
8. What is one of this church's most important contributions to your life?
9. What causes you to stay at this church?
10. What is one of this church's most important contributions to our community?
11. What makes our church distinctive?

Future (20 minutes)
12. What should we focus on in the next five years?
13. If you had a magic wand, what would you change about our church?

Wrap-Up (10 minutes)
Thank everyone for coming and sharing. Remind them that this is the first step in the church's long-range planning process, which was approved by the governing body. The next step, after all the small groups have met, will be to share this material with the long-range planning committee to help them with their visioning process. Tell them when the long-range planning com-

49

mittee will have its first meeting and when its report is scheduled to be given to the governing body (about a year from now).

The Long-Range Planning Committee

Ask the official body of your church to create a task force that will develop a five-year plan for ministry. You might call it the "Joel committee" in honor of the prophet who proclaimed that our young would see visions and our old would dream dreams (Joel 2:28). You could preach a great sermon or sermon series on this! Divide the task force into four subgroups: worship, programming, staff, and building. Choose one person to chair the overall project, one person as vice-chair of the overall project, one person to chair each subgroup, and as many persons as you want to serve on each subgroup (perhaps six to eight). You may want to serve as a member of each subgroup, or you may want to serve only on the overall project as a member.

Have the subgroups meet over a series of months. In their first meeting, they should evaluate where the church has been in the past in their particular area. For example, the worship team may want to discuss how worship has changed over the years at your church. Each group should also ask someone to serve as recorder or secretary to keep notes. This will make it easier to stay on track between meetings and assist in pulling together the final report.

At the second meeting, they should discuss what is being done in worship now. What do they like best about it? What seems to not be working well? Let them also identify some churches similar to yours that have successfully handled similar challenges. Let them plan to visit some of these churches to bring back ideas that might be applicable in your situation. You might also be able to put some books in their hands or direct them to some internet resources that deal positively with the challenges they are identifying.

At their third meeting, they might make recommendations about what they would like to see done in worship in the future.

At their fourth meeting, they would review their suggestions and make a timeline for these things. For example, they may say that in the past there was a children's moment in the eleven o'clock service. This was discontinued three years ago because there were no children present. There are children now, and a children's time should be started within the next three months. The building subgroup may say that the last time we added onto our building was in 1963, and we have grown a lot since then. They may say they recommend forming a building committee within six months to present a proposal to the church for a new building within the next year.

When its work is completed, each subgroup presents its recommendations to the full committee. The full committee draws up a document outlining the recommendations—with dates for completion—for each area. The document is then be presented to the official church governing body for approval.

Sample Timeline for Long-Range Planning

Here is a sample timeline for the long-range planning committee. Adapt it to fit your needs. After your church council approves it, you could publicize it in your newsletter.

January—Church governing body approves the long-range planning process, which begins with small group listening sessions. The governing body also appoints a committee to nominate the chair, vice chair, four team chairs (worship, programming, staffing, and buildings), and the team members.
March—Church governing body approves nominees for long-range planning process.
April–May—Listening sessions with the congregation in small groups are held.
April—Long-range planning (Joel) committee meets to discuss the church's mission statement. [The pastor has supplied the committee with several statements from other churches that he

thinks might be useful. The pastor has prayed about this mission statement and has spent time talking with other church leaders about it, individually. The statement must be short enough to be memorized. Better yet, it should be short enough to fit on a T-shirt or letterhead. Bill Hybel's book *Courageous Leadership* (Grand Rapids, MI: Zondervan, 2002), has a great section on mission statements.]

May—Joel committee finalizes recommendation for mission statement and presents it to church governing body for consideration.

June—Joel committee subgroups meet to evaluate the church's past. Church governing body approves and/or amends mission statement.

July—Joel committee subgroups meet to evaluate church's present. [George Bullard, *Pursuing the Full Kingdom Potential of Your Congregation* (St. Louis, MO: Lake Hickory Resources, 2005), 72–74: lists ten questions for generative dialogue that would be helpful.]

August—Joel committee subgroups meet to establish long-range goals (five years).

September—Joel committee subgroups meet to refine long-range goals and begin work on mid-range goals that will carry the church toward the accomplishment of long-range goals.

October—Joel committee subgroups meet to refine and finalize mid-range goals.

November—Joel committee group chairs meet to blend each of the four areas' long-range and mid-range goals into one document. Each goal has a recommended date of completion.

December—Joel committee releases report to church governing body for study.

January—Church governing body accepts/amends Joel committee report

When the final Joel committee report is approved, it would be great to preach on it for several Sundays. Perhaps you will preach on each subcommittee's vision. As you prepare the worship services, and as you talk with church members about this road map, take time to become aware of what it will taste, smell, sound, and feel like. Weave into this vision the taste of meals served in your new kitchen, the savor of nourishing food offered to homeless families. Hear the laughter of children playing on the new playground or the sound of the new music equipment. Conjure the acrid smell of asphalt being poured or the aroma of fresh pine lumber as your new building addition goes up. Make them feel the joy of a profound connection within a new small group, or help them hear the sound of your growing youth group pounding across new gymnasium floors.

Conclusion

Now that we have a destination and a road map for getting there, it is time to talk about mobilizing lay volunteers to implement this plan.

5

Leading and Managing Volunteers

Volunteers who are filled with the Spirit of God are the lifeblood of the church. They want to do work they feel is significant, at a time that is convenient, under conditions that are supportive. This chapter discusses ways the pastor can facilitate these conditions.

A Theological Focus for Leading and Managing Volunteers

When I think about the ministry of Jesus, one thing astonishes me most, and I am filled with greater wonder at this thing with each passing year of my life. It is not that he was born of a virgin, that he gave his life for our salvation, or even that he rose from the dead. These things fill me with gratitude, awe, and praise; but they do not surprise me.

I am not surprised so much by what God can do in Christ Jesus. I am surprised by what God has chosen to do in, and through, us. Jesus was physically present to recruit, train, and lead his followers for about three years. After that, he was able to turn everything over to ordinary men and women who were led and empowered by his Spirit. That's it. Three years, and then the training wheels were off for eternity. We often see the humorous quip that is supposed to be uttered as a warning from our heavenly Father, "Don't make me come down there." But sometimes I wonder, how can God resist? It is astonishing to me that God chooses to work through people like you and me to manifest his work and mission. Even more surprising is that this plan works!

Part of the redemption process is that when we are born again, or regenerated, the Holy Spirit equips each of us with gifts for ministry (1 Corinthians 12). The doctrine of the priesthood of all believers reminds us that even though few are called to ordained ministry, all baptized persons are called to ministry within the priesthood of believers. Baptism is a commissioning into the ministry of the laity. Part of our role as ordained ministers is to help our people find effective ways of exercising their spiritual gifts for ministry. To do this, we engage in a process of invitation, training, goal setting, implementation, evaluation, and celebration.

Invitation

Most churches have a team of church members who nominate the church's lay leadership. In The United Methodist Church, this team is called the committee on lay leadership. The pastor chairs this team, whose task it is to nominate people to serve in various official capacities. Those who are nominated by this committee are then contacted by a committee member and invited to serve. If they agree to do so, their nomination is approved by the charge conference or sometimes by the church ouncil.

When the pastor chairs a meeting, it is good to start on time and end about fifty minutes later if possible. Even if important people have not yet arrived, it is a good idea to start politely anyway. There should be an agenda printed and handed out, but there should be room on the agenda for team members to bring up their concerns. An agenda generally makes people feel more comfortable by letting them know what to expect.

Inviting, or recruiting, laypersons to exercise leadership should involve four components: vision for ministry, job description, giftedness, and significance. The first and most important factor is our Church's vision for ministry. It has been said that if we don't know where we want to go, any road will get us there. Many churches are ineffective in their ministry because they do not understand what their target or goal is. As you move through the process described in the last chapter, your congregations will focus with laser-like clarity on their vision, purpose, and goals for ministry. If this vision has been cast so that the entire congregation can grasp it, your task of recruitment will be far easier. If your congregation understands the vision of ministry, which together you are moving toward, the committee on lay leadership will have a good idea of the kind of person you will need to recruit to lead that ministry area.

Once persons are identified, **tell them that they have been nominated by the committee.** It is affirming for people to know that a group of their fellow members see in them the giftedness and maturity to be entrusted with leadership. Tell the person what the job is and how it fits in with the church's overall vision for ministry. Help the person see clearly how their team's ministry will be an important component in reaching the overall goal.

The pastor does not need to be the only person to recruit leaders. In most churches, the members of the committee on lay leadership contact many of the persons nominated. The pastor and the committee should use their best judgment as to who should contact the nominees. But it would be useful for the pastor to share the four steps of an invitation to serve with the rest of the committee, so that everyone can learn how to do this important ministry well.

Second, **share the job description and budget with the nominees.** It would be ideal to have thought-out job descriptions written up for the positions. If you don't have them, you can just let the nominees know what is expected of them. If they are expected to attend council meetings bimonthly, let them know. If they are expected to recruit or lead a team, tell them how the recruitment of their team is to be carried out. Share with the nominees your vision for what this team could accomplish. This is also a good time to share with them the annual budget for their ministry teams. Explain to them how much is available on a monthly basis, as well as on an annual basis, and the procedure your church uses for accessing and disbursing those funds. For example, your church may have $1,200 budgeted for children's ministries, but only 1/12 of that may be available each month. It may also be that before any money is spent or reimbursed, a purchase order has to be issued. Whatever your church's policy, now is the time to explain it. If you wait until they actually take office, they may have have spent a considerable amount of their own money, expecting to be reimbursed. If they have made incorrect assumptions, it could be embarrassing for everyone.

Third, you will want to **discuss with them their giftedness for this particular ministry.** Tell them why you, or the nominating team, thought they would be well suited for this ministry opportunity. Ask them what they see as their gifts and abilities in this area.

Finally, **share with them the significance of this work**. You are asking them to donate time that they could otherwise be spending earning money, playing with their children, relaxing, or doing any number of other things they find meaningful. Why is this work we are asking them to do more meaningful than all these other things? Help them get a vision of the far-reaching value of their leadership. If you are asking them to lead a team of people to take up the pew registration pads each Sunday, don't just leave it at that. Help them see how this task fits in with your church's mission to transform lives. Remind them that those pads contain the contact information for visitors, who would like to find a new way to connect with God and the church. Perhaps a visitor is going through a very difficult time in her life and a connection with this church would be a lifeline for her. Those pew pads are the vital first link in that lifeline. The truth is that all of our work in ministry can seem mundane, routine, and repetitive. We all need to be refreshed and reminded of the significance of the routine service we offer.

At my first church out of seminary, I was prevailed on to direct the choir. One day I was at the home of the organist, who was a retired schoolteacher. She was an extremely polite lady. After we had spent about an hour working together on a piece of music, she looked at me as though she had just discovered the missing piece of a puzzle and said, "You think I have nothing more important to do than work on this music!" I replied, "No indeed, but I think we both feel that no one has anything more important to do than to serve and glorify God." We resumed our work.

Many clergy find it difficult to ask others who are busy with family and work responsibilities to take on significant roles in ministry. A balance of work, family, worship, ministry, and recreation is important for everyone, including the pastor. But we should stay in touch with the reality that the work that all of us do for the cause of Christ has eternal significance, which will never lose its reward or value. It is part of our calling to help our people realize the significance of the ministry they do. Their lives could devolve into a meaningless round of work, responsibility, and pleasure. It is our task to lift their heads and help them see the eternal significance of what they do for Jesus Christ, who gave his life on Calvary for us all.

Job Descriptions

It is helpful to have written job descriptions for each job in your church. Many are available from the denomination, and you can order copies of them. However, there are many other jobs in our churches for which there may be no denominational descriptions. It would be helpful for your churches to create their own.

If your church needs job descriptions, perhaps the first thing is to decide who will lead this task. Discuss it with your committee on lay leadership or nominations. See what they recommend, and then refer their recommendation to the governing body, such as the church council. Let the council then approve a team of people to pull together the job descriptions. In doing so, it would be a good idea to ensure that these job descriptions dovetail with any denominational guidelines. Also, it would be helpful to consult with others in your congregation who have done this job in the past. When the task is complete, present the information to the council for review; amendments and approval would be in order at the next meeting.

Identifying Giftedness and Leadership

The nominations committee, or the committee on lay leadership, should provide a means of identifying the spiritual gifts and abilities of the membership. Your committee should decide how they want to do this. They could distribute surveys in Sunday school classes, in worship, or through the mail. There are many surveys and questionnaires available to help people identify their spiritual gifts. You could call your denominational bookstore and get several good recommendations. With the permission of your laypeople, keep a copy of the score sheets from the spiritual gift inventories. It would be helpful if you created a running list matching gifts with parishioners' names. For example, you might write the heading "Evangelism" and then list the names of everyone who is gifted in evangelism. Do this with each gift, and you will have a good pool of people to select from when you are in the nominations process.

In addition to identifying giftedness, you need to learn who your real leaders are. As you know, some of your leaders have important official positions in the church, and some of them are nearly invisible. If you have been in your parish for several years, you have already figured out who the leaders are; but if you are relatively new, a great way to find out who the leaders are is to ask. There are a lot of good ways to ask; I have two favorites. The first way is to ask people in the congregation as I am visiting with them one on one. The other way is to put a brief questionnaire in the bulletin, to be filled out during the service and placed in the collection plate. I don't usually say I am trying to find out who the leaders are; I just say I am trying to get to know the congregation. Here are the questions I like to ask:

1) If there were an important question involving the church's ministry to children or youth, whose counsel would you seek in addition to the counsel of the pastor?
2) If there were an important question involving ministry to adults, whose counsel would you seek?
3) If there were an important question involving the building facilities, whose counsel would you seek?
4) If there were an important question involving the church's budget, whose counsel would you seek?
5) If you had a personal crisis, and needed a wise Christian friend to pray with and counsel you, who would it be?
6) If you were to name five leaders in our congregation, who would they be?

The names that come up most frequently are the real leaders in your church, whether they are serving on ministry teams or not. These are the people whose permission and approval is needed to move any ministry initiative forward. As much as you can, keep the lines of communication open with them (talk to them at least once per quarter) and heed their advice. Unfortunately, it is unlikely that they will all speak with the same voice, so it is your leadership task to figure out what these leaders want, establish common ground, and then lead in that direction with their voice in your ear.

Training, Feedback, and Appreciation

Once a person has been nominated and approved for a ministry leadership position, it is important to see that they receive training. Fortunately, many of the people nominated will have had this particular position before; they already have experience. If that is the case, they may not need training as such, but they still might appreciate the opportunity to improve their skills.

There are several ways you can train leaders or help them hone their skills. One is by arranging for them to meet with the person who has done this ministry previously. It also might be helpful to have them meet with someone who fills this ministry function in a neighboring church you admire. You could also order denominational materials that are designed for this purpose. There are also denominational workshops that are specifically designed for training the lay leadership.

Sometimes it is a good idea for the pastor to train the workers. For example, if there is no one else who can do an excellent job of training, and if it is a position that is important enough for you to make time to offer the training, it would be useful for you to work with them closely until they feel comfortable in the new role. Remember that some people desire close interaction, and others prefer to work it out for themselves.

Perhaps the best way to train leaders is with a combination of feedback and appreciation. Call them and ask how the work is going. If they are open to it, help them decide what their next steps might be. Just knowing that you, or another competent staff member, are available increases their comfort, their confidence, and their feelings of being appreciated. Call them by name when you see them. Consider sending them birthday cards. Affirm what they are doing. If they need more money for their ministry next year, try to help them get it put into the budget.

It is also important and powerful to express sincere thanks. An e-mail or a phone call, just to say thank you and for no other reason, is affirming and encouraging. (Remember, if you process any other business during the phone call, other than thanking them, they will probably not view it as a call to thank them; they will likely view it as a call to process more of your agenda, with a polite prelude of thanks. This principle is also true when calling to see how someone is doing after an illness or difficult time. If you move on to any other business during the call, the person will assume that the other business was the *real* reason for your call.) Even better is a handwritten note of just a few sentences. It takes about ten minutes to write a note, but this simple gesture can affirm a person's faith in the church as an institution and release a great deal of renewed energy for serving Jesus Christ. People need to be quietly and sincerely thanked. Writing one note each day may be the most powerful ten minutes of the pastor's day.

Goal Setting

In your long-range plan, you will identify long-range and mid-range goals. That is, you will have articulated where you would like to be in two, three, and five years. One of the first priorities for each ministry team is to establish short-term goals that will make it possible to reach the mid-range goals. For example, perhaps the long-term goal of the outreach group is to go on a foreign mission trip in five years. The mid-range goal may be to identify where that trip will be, what kind of mission it will be, and who will go. Short term goals might be:

1) Invite three speakers who have been on short-term foreign missions to address the outreach group this year. These invitations should be extended, accepted, and calendared by February 28.
2) Designate a fund-raiser for the mission trip, with a target of raising $2,000. We recommend that it be repeated each year until the mission trip is taken. Ideas for the fund-raiser will be discussed in February and March, chosen by March 31, and executed by October 31.
3) Invite a denominational representative to address our group on possible short-term missions, so we can decide where we would like to go. This will be done during the summer. By December 31, we will decide where we want to go.

Notice that these short-term goals all contribute to the achievement of the long- and mid-range goals. Also, each of them has a target date for completion. It would be a good idea to have a ministries planning retreat either in November or in January, so that each team could make its plans, and its budget recommendations, for the coming year. If we have the retreat (which could last a half day, a day, or a weekend) in November, we could have incoming and outgoing members meet together to make the plans. This would provide continuity. It would also mean that we could get started immediately on the execution of our plans in January. However, November may be too busy in some churches to plan the retreat during that month. In any case, the team will need to make its budget recommendations for the coming year to the finance committee well before the end of the current year.

Implementation

I have found that the best way to get team ministry done is to have regularly scheduled times for teams to meet. For instance, teams may want to meet monthly, bimonthly, or quarterly. It is a good idea to pick a day and a time for the regular meeting, for instance the first Monday of each quarter at seven in the evening. Even though people know the regular time for the meeting, they will still need personal reminders in addition to bulletin and newsletter announcements. Consider asking the chair to do this. Some churches have the secretary do this. If you have good action plans with completion dates and regularly scheduled meetings, implementation will happen naturally; but if you just meet "when something comes up" not much will happen.

You will probably need to use different leadership styles with different ministry teams. For example, some teams are probably functioning really well, and may just need you to say, "Thanks. You are doing a great job!" Other teams may be nearly defunct and need you to come alongside to help them restructure their approach to ministry. Still other teams may need you to serve as a resource person, feeding them great materials and fresh approaches. The balance you are looking for is to offer as much help as the team finds helpful. Leadership style and intensity reminds me of using fertilizer on a vegetable garden. Without any fertilizer, the vegetables will probably survive the summer, but bear little. With too much fertilizer, the plants will die quickly. With the right amount of fertilizer, there will be healthy plants and an abundant yield. It takes trial and error to get the proportions right, but when in doubt, use a little less. As one of my seminary professors used to say, "Helpfulness is helpful only if it is *perceived* as being helpful."

Not only is it helpful to use different leadership styles with different ministry teams, it is helpful to coordinate our leadership style with the individual leader we are dealing with. One of the basic truths of human bonding is that we feel most comfortable with people who are like ourselves. Someone who always seems deliberate, steady, and risk-averse (think: accountants) will not be inclined to trust the leadership of someone who comes across as fiery, impassioned, and risk-taking (think: prophets). If we can learn to have compassion (to feel what others are feeling) for the people we are talking with one on one, we can be more successful in communicating and sharing leadership with them. In 1986, Tony Robbins published an interesting book called *Unlimited Power*. He creates a lot of hype, but his insights into communicating effectively and creating rapport with others are solid gold.

Implementation Through Technology, Especially in Multi-church Charges

Technology has opened up vast new possibilities for lay leadership and service, which can be done off-site. Since multi-church charges may have no staff, but relatively high total membership, the pastor tends to focus more on functions of preaching, administrating things of major importance, and visiting parishioners in extreme circumstances. Multi-church charges and start-up churches have little money for staff, and they frequently do not have offices, so it is a boon for them to use technology to their advantage.

Technology is great for the pastor who may not have a church office. Virtual offices can cut down on long commutes between churches, and because of internet technology, pastors do not necessarily have to have secretaries in adjoining offices. For example, the pastor could e-mail the material for the church bulletin to the secretary or to the worship leader for the projections. Also, a volunteer could do the newsletter quite effectively without setting foot on the church campus. Contributors to the newsletter could e-mail their articles to the editor, who could then compile them and e-mail them, or place them on the church website for the members to download. This means that volunteers can do church work when they have spare time, and pastors can do work for multi-church charges even when they cannot travel to the physical location. It also cuts down on postage and paper expenses, as well as labor.

Church websites, which can be maintained remotely, can also become virtual spaces for community. Not only can information and announcements be posted on the website, but the church can also purchase software that will enable the church to host chat rooms and discussion groups. For example, you could have a virtual discussion group concerning worship planning. People could go to the website, see where the conversation is heading, and post their ideas. This works well when it is difficult for people to get together physically. It also has a certain "coolness factor" that many young adults enjoy. A word of caution: websites must be maintained regularly. Out-of-date websites make churches appear neglected and poorly led. This reflects on the pastor, as well as the congregation.

There are many technologically efficient ways to implement the church's ministry. Phone trees can be a great way to get your messages out to the congregation. Announcements for meetings can be e-mailed or relayed by phone tree quicker than making a dozen phone calls or writing a dozen post cards. Church treasurers and financial secretaries can do their work remotely, using financial software.

Conclusion: Evaluation and Celebration

The annual planning retreat is a great time to refocus the lay leadership on the long-term goals and mission statement of the church. This could come first on the agenda at the planning retreat, which would be a good time to evaluate the effectiveness of the teams' ministries during the past year. Each team could discuss:

What were our goals this year?
How did they tie in with our long-range plan?
How did they tie in with our mission statement?
Did we implement our goals?
What accounted for our successes?
How could we have improved our effectiveness?
Were we comfortable working within our budgeted financial resources?

This part of the planning retreat would naturally come early on the day's agenda. After each work area or team has had a chance to do self-evaluation, it would be wonderful to let them report their answers to the above questions. A celebratory meal, or festive refreshments, would be a nice time of affirmation and celebration before moving on to plan the next year's ministry plans.

In his list of eight things leaders do, Jack Welch says, "Leaders celebrate" (Jack Welch, *Winning* [New York: HarperBusiness, 2005], 63). If you can brainstorm a great way to celebrate the year's ministries and a way to publicly thank the people who made them happen, that would be powerful. The challenge is in figuring out a way to do this that is not a burden on the very people you are trying to honor. Perhaps you could have a Sunday morning or a Sunday evening when you have a parade of ministries. Bill Hybels talks about this in his book on leadership. It might be fun to have the people who are involved in each ministry come forward and let a spokesperson read a brief statement of what they did. It would be wise for you to see all the "brief" statements in writing, ahead of time, to ensure that they fit in your allotted time frame. Just imagine how large your attendance would be on that Sunday and how excited everyone would be. Maybe a potluck or an ice cream social would be great afterwards.

6

Managing Your Building and Safety Systems

Most of us are in ministry because we genuinely care about others. We want to nurture and strengthen them, and bless them with the Spirit's gifts of love, peace, and joy. Building and safety systems are probably no one's idea of fun, but they do provide important safeguards for those whom we most want to bless. By putting policies and systems in place, we protect people from physical danger, and facilities are available for all to use as intended. Well-maintained facilities are attractive to visitors and are a valuable tool as we make disciples.

Trustees or Building and Grounds Committees

Most churches have a committee established to take responsibility for the church's physical plant. In The United Methodist Church, this is the board of trustees. We can read about the trustee's responsibilities in the *Book of Discipline*. As with the staff - parish relations committee, the pastor does not have a vote on the board of trustees.

The trustees are the committee responsible for the church's physical plant; they also handle bequests. This is a great help to the pastor in two ways. First, we automatically have a team set up to care for the church's physical plant; and second, we have a team that handles some rather sticky situations for us. As with any team in the church, there is no point in the pastor attempting to force new ideas down their throats; but most trustees would appreciate the pastor's sharing with them some of the ideas found in this chapter. The suggestions found here are not necessarily things that every church should do, but are good things for churches to consider.

Securing the Building

Who unlocks the building and locks up after meetings? Even if our church has a full-time sexton, there are many meetings that occur when the sexton is off duty. Sometimes a trustee is in the habit of locking up after meetings he attends. Otherwise, if a staff member will attend the meeting, it makes sense for the staff member to unlock and lock the building. The staff member should unlock the building about twenty to thirty minutes in advance of the meeting, turn on lights, and adjust the thermostat if needed. Often people arrive early for meetings, and it annoys these influential, volunteer leaders to have to sit in the car and wait for the staff member to come flying in at the last minute, appearing irresponsible and unprepared. It is wise leadership for the staff member to be the first to arrive and among the last to leave, because she is available to transact business with everyone who comes. Besides, some of the most important conversations happen before and after meetings; we don't want to exclude ourselves from these. They are the conversations that keep the pastor in the loop. This may add almost an hour to the time it takes to lead a meeting, but it is an hour well spent.

If the meeting is at night, and the neighborhood seems unsafe, the staff person may want to wait in the car until there is someone of the same sex to walk in with. The staff person may also want to ask someone of the same sex to accompany her to the parking lot after the meeting. If you cannot get someone of the same sex to accompany you, then you will want to get at least two persons to accompany you.

Before leaving, the staff person is wise to check every door, even doors we think were not used during the course of our meeting. If there is a robbery with access gained through an unlocked door, responsibility will inevitably be placed directly on the last person to secure the building.

Locking Up After Services

Often the pastor arrives quite early on Sunday mornings and is exhausted by the time services are over. Since trustees are always present at services, it makes sense for them to take turns locking up after church. If you have a system that everyone is happy with, there is no reason to change it. But if you are stuck locking up every Sunday, why not consider asking the trustees if they would take responsibility for this? The chair of trustees could assign each trustee a Sunday to lock up and send out the assignments six months or a year in advance. If a trustee knows that she will not be present, she can trade with another trustee. If you are the still the last person to leave, that is OK; all you have to do is turn off your light and set the alarm on your way out.

Keys

Who has a key to your church? Unfortunately, many churches are unsure about the answer to this question. Over the years, different church officers may have been given keys. They may have had them duplicated and given the duplicates to friends or family. If you suspect this is the case, here is a common sense solution. Have the board of trustees draw up a list of everyone who should have keys. Have the trustees place a repeating notice in the bulletin or newsletter that, on a certain date, the locks on the church will be rekeyed. Include a list of job titles (not the names)

71

of the people who will be issued new keys. Let people know that if they feel they need a key on a permanent basis and they are not on the list they should send a request to the trustees. Send a letter to each person who should have a key, informing them of the change, and tell them how they can get their new key. If possible, have all the door locks keyed the same, so that one key opens all the exterior doors. Have a certain number of keys made, for example, twenty. Have the keys numbered one through twenty, with the words "Do Not Duplicate" on them. Make an inventory list of the twenty keys that includes who was issued the key, the number of the key, the office of the key holder (pastor, trustees chair, choir director, and so on), date issued, and date returned. Keep a couple of spares to loan out, but keep a record of who borrows them. Perhaps the church secretary could maintain the list. It is reasonable to repeat this process every five to ten years.

Alarms

Many churches have alarm systems. These are much to be desired, particularly if the system includes motion detectors. Thieves no longer seem concerned about desecrating a house of God. To the contrary, some prefer them as an easy mark. In addition, sanctuaries sometimes are purposefully desecrated by hate groups. An effective alarm system, with motion detectors, can prevent thieves from having time to do a great deal of mischief. Motion detectors are important because vandals may not enter through a door.

Alarms also provide a good backup system if the wrong person procures a key or if a vandal enters through an unsecured window or door. The best systems will not only make a piercing sound, but will also connect directly to a monitoring station. It is desirable to have a system that common thieves cannot cut or disconnect before entering. It is also far easier to change the code on the alarm system than to change keys. Often it can be arranged so that each person has her own code. It is useful to place a sign-in pad beside the alarm keypad, so that people in the building after hours can sign in and out. This way, you avoid setting the alarm with someone left in the building.

Maintenance

At least once each year, it is useful to have the trustees make an inspection of the building, inside and out. They should note the things that need repair or refurbishment, prioritize their list, and set about getting the repairs made. If the repairs exceed their budget, they should address their concerns to the finance committee or church council before overspending their line item. Sometimes, such as in the case of a heater or air-conditioning unit going out, this may involve emergency meetings. So be it. It is better to have the inconvenience of an emergency meeting than to have large, unbudgeted purchases made without the approval of the church council.

Once each year, the trustees chair, staff-parish relations committee chair, and parsonage committee chair should also inspect the parsonage inside and out, to address needed repairs. Since the work of the trustees involves not only mechanical systems such as heating systems, but also aesthetics such as paint, carpet, and landscaping, it is wise to have a few influential persons of excellent taste on the board, even if they know nothing about mechanical systems. I once had a board of trustees that replaced the beautiful wooden front door of the sanctuary with a hideously inappropriate door of glass and steel. These trustees were effective problem solvers, but had no sense of aesthetics.

The trustees are also responsible for seeing that there is sufficient insurance coverage for all contingencies, including damage to the buildings, and liability for accidents and staff malpractice. This insurance coverage should be evaluated each year. If there is a disaster, and the church is not sufficiently insured, the responsibility will rest secondarily with the trustees and primarily with the pastor who did not ensure that the trustees had done their job. Similarly, it is crucial to have anything repaired immediately that might cause an accident. This includes items like wobbly handrails, frayed electrical cords, loose carpet, or rotting floor-boards. You would never want someone to have an accident due to negligence on your part. If you see something dangerous, inform the chair of trustees and make a note of having done so. Schedule a time to follow up to see if the item is repaired.

Building Use

Louise Jones wants to use the church fellowship hall for bingo every Thursday night. Admission is charged, prizes are awarded, and the games are open only to people whom Mrs. Jones personally approves. It is a private game.

Catherine Swartz is a representative for a popular weight-loss organization who sees an opportunity to increase her profits. She is an influential member of the church who is asking to have her meetings in the fellowship hall every Tuesday night.

Jim Johnson is not a member of the church. He wants to have Alcoholics Anonymous meetings in the education building every Monday night. He prefers that no other meetings be held that night, in order to enhance the sense of anonymity.

Jennie Alvarez is from California. She is living locally for a year and is a member of a United Methodist church back home, but you have never met her. She has called to say she wants to have her wedding in your church because it is so pretty.

Allison Smith is the daughter of the chair of trustees. She wants to have her son's fifth birthday party in the church fellowship hall because all those kids would mess up her house. Besides, the church playground is so nice. Although others have asked, no one has been allowed to do this before.

Cindy Slater's wedding is scheduled for tomorrow. Her mother and father came in today to remove the pulpit and altar table to make room for all the flowers. They used nails to attach bouquets and candles to the pews. The disc jockey has set up his equipment in the sanctuary so he can supply the bridal couple's favorite hit tunes as the prelude. They plan to serve champagne at the reception in the fellowship hall.

George Kerr has a piece of land that he has realized is useless and unmarketable, and he would like to donate it to the church. He is tired of paying the taxes on it.

Gertrude Hales would like to give $250,000 in memory of her late husband. The money is to be used to install a new stained glass window behind the altar.

If you wait to establish building policies until Louise Jones or Catherine Swartz are knocking on the door of the parsonage, asking if it is OK to have bingo or weight-loss meetings in the church fellowship hall, you might as well shut the door and call U-Haul, because it will get ugly. Before Louise or Catherine come knocking on your door, why not ask your trustees to establish or update the building use policy? This is the time for the pastor to use his influence in shaping the policy, before specific personalities become involved. Is it OK for for-profit groups to use our facilities? Is it OK for support groups to meet on our premises when no one else is there? Is the church available for the weddings of nonmembers? Is the fellowship hall available for showers, anniversary parties, and birthday parties? Can church equipment, such as tables and chairs, be loaned out? If so, what are the conditions? What is the fee schedule, if any? All these things should be spelled out clearly in a building use policy that is worded kindly and positively, clearly connecting the policy to the stated mission and values of the church. This policy should be displayed prominently on a church bulletin board, and copies of it should be given to members who wish to use the facilities. If there is any doubt about the interpretation, it is good to send these persons, without comment, to the board of trustees for clarification, making it clear that they, and not the pastor, will make the determination. If use of the building or facilities is requested and approved, it should be scheduled on the church's master calendar, along with all other meetings, to ensure there is no problem with double booking.

A booklet that outlines the policies for weddings is useful. This booklet should clarify any gray areas you can foresee, including a fee schedule for use of the building, a list of the church personnel who must be used (wedding director, sexton, pastor, musicians), and their fees, if any. It should clarify any limitations on decorations or moving of furniture. Policies should express clearly any prohibitions concerning rice, flower petals on the carpet, alcohol, secular music, and so on. No pastor wants to get between a bride and her dream wedding. Let the secretary hand a prospective bride the little bridal booklet, clarifying that these policies were set in place by the trustees with the approval of the church council. Go over this booklet with the nuptial couple at your first meeting with them.

The trustees are charged with the responsibility of deciding whether to accept gifts and bequests. There is little doubt that George Kerr will be displeased with the trustees' decision to reject his gift of useless land; perhaps they can word their rejection tactfully. It is equally likely that Gertrude Hales will be offended if the trustees reject her offer to install a new window above the altar. It is fortunate that the trustees make these decisions, leaving the pastor out of the fray. The wise pastor will remain out of it.

It is also worth addressing other questions of safety and access in terms of building policy. For example, should the church doors be left unlocked and unattended during office hours? Is this a safe procedure for staff? Should some sort of intercom system be installed? How are vagrants, homeless, and the needy handled? Is there a policy that vagrants are to be addressed only if there is more than one person in the building? Are the staff and volunteers comfortable with the procedures now in place? Are computers frequently backed up in case of theft? Are computers and copiers in locked rooms and encoded so they cannot be improperly accessed? Is there a policy for inclement weather? Is there a plan in case of fire or natural disaster?

Protecting People From Abuse

It is a terrible tragedy when persons are abused in God's own house. It is no less a tragedy when leaders are falsely accused of doing so. It is important to have systems in place that protect everyone, as much as possible, from abuse, injury, or false accusation. For this reason, it is advisable to do background checks on all persons dealing directly with children or youth, particularly if these persons are new to your community. Background checks are no longer viewed as an extreme measure of security; they have become a matter of due diligence. Parents will appreciate knowing that this precaution has been taken and, should the unthinkable happen, the pastor and trustees will not be guilty of having been asleep at the wheel. If your trustees need help with this, consider asking a local judge or lawyer to address your trustees on the subject. I guarantee they will not tell the trustees just to forget about it. While it is true that your church probably never "did it this way before," it is also true that people did not use to sue churches in cases of abuse.

There are many publications and workshops available that deal with the subject of creating a safe environment for children. It would be well for us, and our children's leaders, to master this information. In this brief space, I will boil it down to this: ensure that no adult is ever alone with one child or youth. Further, no adult should ever be alone with a group of young children.

No adult should be alone with a child or youth under any circumstances, because this puts both persons at risk. The only exception would be if the adult were the parent or close relative of the child. The lone child or youth may be at risk of being abused in some way; the adult is at risk of being accused of abusing the child or youth. Suffice it to say that if a child or youth even raises a hint of a complaint against an adult with whom she was alone, the adult is presumed guilty and cannot possibly prove her innocence. Being alone with a child or youth is like peering over the edge of Sheol. It is dangerous, and just the specter of it should be thoroughly terrifying.

Several years ago we had an unfortunate situation in our nursery that mildly illustrates this point. Our paid nursery worker was the only adult in the nursery; her helper did not arrive as scheduled. One of the children in the nursery was new, and when the parent came to pick him up, the child was fretful. The parent began to interrogate the child. Finally, the parent asked, "Did the nursery worker hit you?" The child nodded his head "yes."

No one will ever know whether our nursery worker hit that child. I think it highly unlikely, because this employee was impeccable in every way. But this created no small stir in our children's department and made parents think twice about entrusting us with their children. We also placed our employee in a terribly unfair position by leaving her alone with the children. One can only imagine what would have happened if the parent had asked, "Did the nursery worker touch your private place?" Now we have a policy firmly and clearly in place that no one is to be alone in a room with small children. If children must be taken to the bathroom or changed, the door is left wide open, and another adult is within earshot.

It is not always polite or convenient to adhere to this policy. For example, if we could not get two persons in the nursery, we simply would not offer nursery care on that day. Nor do we allow youth workers to pick up or drop off youth if it means that at some point the adult will be alone in the car with one youth. However, once the parents understand the policy and the reasons for it, they appreciate our prudent care.

For similar reasons, we have placed windows in every classroom door. We prefer to have the doors open. We also have adults who rove the hallways to provide an extra measure of protection. Precautions that are now standard include sign-in/sign-out forms for children in the nursery, requiring parents or designated sponsors to come personally to release their children from elementary-age Sunday school classes, and using permission slips for outings of children and youth. Succinctly worded and clearly displayed sexual harassment policies are also standard precautions intended to protect the denomination in case of suit.

Alone With Parishioners?

These measures also apply to the pastor. When someone comes into my office for a meeting or for counseling, I leave the door ajar and we talk in low tones. Better for the parishioner to feel deprived of a bit of privacy than for the pastor to be accused of an indiscretion against which there is no defense whatsoever. Additionally, it is a good idea to keep a log of what is discussed during counseling sessions. It is not beyond the imagination for an estranged spouse to sue the pastor for "alienation of affection." It used to be that pastors, doctors, and lawyers were the counselors normally sought for advice in complicated matters of the heart and soul. Now, counseling is a profession and discipline of its own. Wise pastors who are not professionally equipped in counseling refer those who are truly troubled to qualified Christian therapists.

It is preferable to avoid being alone with a person of the opposite sex in a ministry setting. Of course, you do not want to express your reservations to the person, for that might make it seem like your motives are not pure or that you do not trust them. When I need to visit a woman, I go when her spouse will be at home. When the appointment is scheduled I say, "I would like to come when Bill will also be there." Sometimes, I simply take a third party with me. I also avoid scheduling counseling appointments at the church with persons of the opposite sex when I know we will be alone. I schedule the appointment at the parsonage, if my wife will be there, or in a public place, such as a restaurant. I have been known to ask the secretary to stay late to provide a third party presence. But whatever happens, I do not meet with women alone.

Unavoidably, there are still times when we, as pastors, find ourselves alone with parishioners. It is useful to be aware that this is extremely dangerous territory, not because we might misbehave, but because we might be perceived by a misguided parishioner as misbehaving. If a parishioner you're visiting with is about eighty years old, the possibility of scandal is diminished. You should not, however, assume that just because you have no sexual interest in a person, or because they are twenty years older than you, that they are "safe." Older persons frequently have fantasies about romantic liaisons with younger persons; every effort should be made to ensure that idle minds and tongues cannot concoct a story about the pastor and the pastor's "friend" alone together.

It is for this same reason that it is unwise for the pastor to remark on a person's physical appearance *in any way*. A parishioner or staff member could shave her head bald, and I would pretend not to notice. A possible exception is if the change in appearance is connected with a serious illness. It is worth remembering that some parishioners of the same sex—as well as the opposite sex—may have secret romantic fantasies or fears about the pastor. You may be able to identify some of these people, but there are others whom you would never suspect. The slightest hint of flirtatious behavior on the pastor's part—including hugs—may be completely misunderstood by the parishioner, throwing them into a world of confusion about the pastor's intentions. The wise pastor seldom initiates hugs. If someone reaches out to hug me in public, I respond only with a very stiff "a-frame" hug, unless it is a moment of tragedy, such as a death. I very seldom hug anyone who could not be mistaken for approaching eighty years of age. I do not get even remotely close enough for a hug if I find myself alone in a room with a person. This is really not a new concept. When I entered the ministry, I read one of my father's books on church administration, which was published in the 1950s. As I recall, the author solemnly intoned: *Any minister who places his hand upon the person of womankind is, in the mildest language I can borrow, an unmitigated fool*. Not much has changed.

7

Managing Your Financial and Reporting Systems

The Leadership Responsibility of Being Informed

The pastor is ultimately responsible for everything that happens in the church. There should be *nothing* he or she does not know, is not abreast of. This is especially true of finances and record keeping. Although the pastor should never handle the church's cash at any time, the pastor should ensure through the finance committee that policies are set and followed for the proper handling of money. If there were ever a mere hint of mishandling of funds, it is likely that your church would decline sharply in attendance and giving, and responsibility would rest with you for having failed to ensure that proper safeguards were both in place and in force. Of all the systems, this may be the least enjoyable for extroverts to administrate, but it is an extremely vulnerable area that must be safeguarded. The good thing is that although oversight in this area requires pastoral leadership, a good system, and vigilance, it requires very little of the pastor's time.

This can be a sensitive subject, especially when we go to a new pastorate and appropriate safeguards and policies are not in place. It could look as though we were impugning the wisdom of the finance committee, or worse, the integrity of those who handle the money. Those who handle money in the church usually have far more clout than an incoming pastor, and these persons can be very intimidating. Nevertheless, if something were to go amiss with the church's finances, the chair of finance would not be held responsible—he is just a volunteer. The blame would be fixed squarely upon the pastor, who is trained, ordained, appointed, and paid to take leadership in ordering the life of the church. Since it is our head on the block, we are wise to ensure that proper procedures for the handling of money are followed.

If you discover that some of the procedures described here are not in place, it usually helps to appeal to a higher authority. Let your financial leaders know that these are not *your* ideas, they are just standard practice in most churches. Show this book, or another on the subject of church finance, to the people on your finance committee. Once they realize that they are out of step, they may decide to make the changes. If push comes to shove, you will have to weigh the risks to your ministry of insisting on policy changes, versus risking financial malfeasance on the part of those who handle the church's money. Just remember, no one ever suspects something is "not right" about the way the church's money is being handled, until it is too late. If you recommend policies to your finance committee that are not accepted and implemented, make your recommendations again in writing, and have them entered into the minutes of the finance committee and the church council. Keep a copy in your files and share a copy with your district superintendent or other supervisory persons. Make a record of your meeting with the D.S. Even if proper policies are not put into place, you will have written and recorded documentation that you fulfilled your leadership obligation with due diligence.

The pastor should know about every aspect of the church's finances. She should know everything the treasurer, financial secretary, and finance chair know. She should know about all regular and special accounts. She should know how much money is in the accounts, where the money came from, where it is held, what it is designated for, and who designated it. She should know what each parishioner has pledged and what each parishioner has given. She should know what obligations the church has to federal, state, and local governments; to the annual conference; to employees for salaries; and so on. This is not to say that the pastor should have the church's budget and financial information memorized—far from it. However, she should be thoroughly familiar with every aspect of the church's financial obligations and be able to put her hands on the all this information quickly. If she is unfamiliar with a new church's system, and has to have the information explained more than once, that is honorable. What is not honorable is to dismiss the information as being too complicated to comprehend. It is our responsibility to know and to lead.

There are pastors who do not want to know what anyone pledges or gives. And there are many parishioners who do not wish the pastor to know how little they give. Nevertheless, the pastor should know everything about the church's business and this includes giving. If the pastor desires to increase the leadership responsibilities of faithful stewards, how will the pastor, who chairs the committee on lay leadership, know who these persons are unless she examines the records of giving? Some who appear to give much, give little. Some who appear to give little, give much. The pastor has a responsibility to know the difference. It is sometimes objected that if the pastor knew who gave what, her pastoral care would be biased. It is fervently to be hoped that this is not so. It is a poor pastor who cannot give spiritual nurture to those of modest means. Nevertheless, both pastor and people make assumptions about who gives generously and who does not. If bias is to enter into pastoral care, it will enter whether the pastor has accurate information or is only guessing; so ignorance is not an effective palliative for ensuring evenhanded pastoral care. It is just ignorance of some very important facts. Additionally, it has been my experience that those who complain most about the church's budget give the impression of being great financial supporters, but in fact give nothing. This knowledge can relieve a lot of unnecessary stress for the pastor.

Even though the pastor knows the pledging and giving records, it creates problems when we speak about this fact publicly. It is good for us to know the giving records, but to say very little about this knowledge. Talking about such things makes people angry and uncomfortable, primarily because many people are embarrassed about their level of giving. People who give little, and who know that the pastor is aware of this fact, tend to assume the pastor neither loves nor respects them. This is hard to overcome.

Notwithstanding the above, there are many outstanding pastors who choose not to know the giving levels of their parishioners. They leave instructions with the financial secretary that if there are any significant changes in a parishioner's giving, to inform the pastor of it. This has certain advantages and ultimately, is a personal leadership choice the pastor must make.

Counting and Depositing Money

The procedures for handling money are not many, but they are important! The principle is that there must always be checks and balances in place, as well as accountability. When the offering is taken up, some churches have it taken immediately to a locked room. Others leave it on the altar until after the service. Whatever method is used, there must be two laypeople involved. (The wise pastor never touches offerings, except perhaps to lift the collection plates in a public prayer of dedication.) The usual method is that the money is placed immediately in bank bags. It is either placed in a safe in the church or deposited immediately in a bank drop. It is not a good idea simply to lock it in the church overnight. And no one should ever take money home with them or lock it in their car. The reason is obvious: if someone should break into one's home or car and steal the money, one would feel personally responsible.

In many churches, the money is taken directly to the church office by two persons after the service. It is then counted with both persons present. A list is made of all contributors and the amounts they gave. According to the *Book of Discipline* (and common sense), these two persons cannot be from the same family. They should rotate frequently on a predetermined basis. This rotation should be a stated and enforced policy of the finance committee. When the money is taken to the bank drop box, the bag should be concealed because it is possible that thieves are watching. There should be several people present when the concealed bag is taken to the car. A second person should follow the one who goes to the bank to make the drop and have a cell phone handy in case of trouble.

The financial secretary keeps a record of each person's contributions. Once a quarter, or at least once a year, this person sends each parishioner a statement of their giving. These statements remind each person of their giving levels and also serve as proof of contributions for tax purposes.

Disbursing Money

Some churches have a business manager who handles the bill paying and payroll. Even if there is a business manager, there is also a treasurer who writes (or signs) the checks. It is useful to require two signatures on all checks; this helps ensure that no one writes a check for private or invalid reasons. The treasurer, or business manager, pays all accounts receivable, meets payroll, handles taxes, and balances the accounts each month. This person also keeps a record of how much money is spent from each line item in the budget. It is ideal if this information is on a computer, using any of several available software programs. Bookkeeping software makes it easier to ensure that the bookkeeping is being handled properly. If a computer program is used, the pastor and the finance chair can receive a monthly statement indicating receipts, overall expenditures, and a line item that shows how much has been spent and how much remains for each budgeted area.

The pastor and the finance chair will want to watch these lines closely to ensure that ministry areas are not overspending their budgets. Some churches have a policy that each ministry area can spend no more than 1/12 of its budget per month. This policy should not be strictly and universally applied since so many expenditures happen seasonally. For example, vacation Bible school spends nearly all its budget between May and July. Nevertheless, the pastor and the finance chair know generally when program expenses traditionally appear and can control spending accordingly. If the pastor sees that the worship work area has spent almost all of its budget by June, she will want to alert the chair of worship to this fact so that spending can be adjusted accordingly. Of course, when someone is given a new job, they are always informed at that time of the budget they have to work with and the procedures for using it.

Some churches use purchase orders. This is a form that is filled out, requesting to buy a certain item. If the purchase is approved, the slip is signed and the check is written. If no purchase order is signed, no reimbursement is given. This is an effective way to control spending, but may not be an effective way to do ministry. Volunteers find it cumbersome to shop for a price on something they need, turn in a purchase order, wait to have it signed, and then return to the store to make the purchase. It seems to work just as well to inform persons of their work area's budget and then to let them know if they are nearing its limits.

Pastors should make it a policy to never touch church cash or offerings. Rather than handle cash, it is better for the pastor and others to do business at stores where the church has an account that is approved for use by certain persons. Alternatively, the pastor could get a check from the treasurer made out in advance for the exact amount. It also is useful to buy whatever is needed and to present receipts for budgeted expenses to the treasurer for reimbursement. Some churches have credit cards for their staff to use. It is important to establish policies for credit card use. These policies should state who may use the card and for what purposes. Personal use of the card is, of course, forbidden.

Audits

Check your denomination's requirements for audits. *The Book of Discipline of The United Methodist Church* requires an annual audit of the church's finances. It is wise to have an outside firm audit the church's books each year. Accountants who are not connected with the church will charge a hefty fee to audit the church's accounts, but this fee will be a lot less than the cost of ongoing inefficiencies and irregularities. It is useful for the finance committee to get an independent assessment of the church's bookkeeping practices. Insisting on an audit also assists in the pastor's and the finance committee's endeavor to practice due diligence. The charge conference forms will ask whether an audit has been done at the end of the year. The *Discipline* does not insist on a professional audit, but this is a wise option.

The Budgeting Process

The budgeting process that many churches use begins in late summer. Each work area is given a statement of what they have budgeted for the current year and a form on which to write their financial needs for the coming year. The staff-parish relations committee (SPRC) meets and recommends salaries. All of this information is sent to the finance committee, who puts together a preliminary budget. This suggested budget is then used in the annual stewardship campaign. Once the campaign is over, the preliminary budget can be adjusted as needed, and approved as final, by the church council.

The Stewardship Campaign

The pastor's leadership in stewardship is crucial. He sets the example of tithing to the church and gently teaches others to follow his example through personal encouragement and challenging sermons. People are curious about whether the pastor puts his money where his mouth is, and they assuredly know what the pastor gives. If we are faithful in stewardship, it strengthens our influence and challenges everyone in the congregation to bring their financial life under the Lordship of Christ. Tithe.

The annual stewardship campaign usually enters the planning stage in midsummer. The stewardship chair and pastor may look at several campaigns that are offered by the denomination or that are used by nationally known congregations. They usually decide together on the program and share this with the finance committee to get feedback before ordering materials.

The basic formula of any campaign involves having some sermons, testimonies, newsletter articles, and letters, all of which deal with stewardship and tithing. About two weeks before commitment Sunday materials are sent to each home in the congregation containing an abbreviated copy of the proposed budget, a letter of appeal, and a pledge card to be returned on or before commitment Sunday. Those who do not pledge receive a polite follow-up letter or call. The pledges are tallied, and these form all or part of the basis for the coming year's budget. Periodic statements are sent in the ensuing year to remind people of the status of their pledge. This is an excellent system that teaches the theology and practice of stewardship and helps churches plan wisely. If you can encourage your church to use this system, it will strengthen it greatly in just a few years.

Working With Your Bookkeeper

One good way the pastor can monitor information is to have financial statements sent to the church, rather than to someone's home. When bank statements and bills arrive, the pastor can look at them to see if she has any questions. For example, unknown to me, our bookkeeper, who appeared quite competent, was not paying the quarterly payroll taxes. When she retired, we found a large stack of registered letters from the IRS, unopened and secreted away! Our church owed tens of thousands of dollars in fines and penalties. Fortunately, we were able to get this resolved. But had I been viewing all the mail before it was put in people's individual mailboxes, I would have seen those registered letters. Now all mail comes to me before it goes to staff mailboxes.

A pastor should get a general feel for what the bookkeeper/office manager does. Talk with her about what she does and the rhythm of her routine. Talk with the treasurer and finance chair about their views on the duties of the bookkeeper/office manager. Do they think this employee is capable and doing a good job? Are there any red flags that either the treasurer or finance chair have seen that indicate the person is not able or willing to fulfill her duties?

A pastor should also take note of the condition of the office of a bookkeeper/office manager. Is the office fairly well-organized? Does clutter build up during busy times, but get put away later; or is the clutter just building up on top of other clutter? Good bookkeepers will always be able to put their hand on a report, even if the office looks to you like it needs work. If the bookkeeper constantly can't seem to find something she knows is in the office or can't seem to make the time to get you the information you need, chances are, she is overwhelmed with day-to-day work. If she is overwhelmed with everyday items, there is no way she will have time to complete quarterly and annual reports.

Federal Reporting Payroll Taxes

Depending on the size of a church, federal payroll taxes (employer and employee Social Security, Medicare, and employee federal tax withholding) are paid semi-weekly, monthly, or quarterly. These taxes may be required to be paid either online or through a bank draft for large payrolls. For smaller payrolls, the taxes can be paid directly to a bank and for very small payrolls, the taxes can be mailed to the IRS with the quarterly 941 form. These reports (Form 941) are always filed on a quarterly basis—due at the end of the month following the end of a quarter (April 30, July 31, October 31, and January 31). Also due on January 31 to the Social Security Administration are copies of the employee W-2 forms for the prior calendar year with a cover sheet that summarizes the W-2s (called a W-3). Churches with large payrolls will be required to submit those forms electronically. Churches with smaller payrolls have the option of submitting electronically.

State Reporting Payroll Taxes

States differ, but not that much. Usually they piggyback the federal requirements. For example, in North Carolina, employee state withholding tax must be submitted to the NC Department of Revenue (NCDR) either semi-weekly, monthly, or quarterly. No additional quarterly report is required. At the end of the calendar year, copies of the W-2s are to be sent to the NCDR along with a top sheet reconciling all state withholding tax payments for the year. Not-for-profit organizations are not required to pay federal unemployment taxes, but some states require them to pay state unemployment taxes.

State Reporting Sales Tax

Some states require not-for-profit organizations to collect and remit sales tax on merchandise sales. This would include sales of Christmas ornaments, mugs, cookbooks, and other items through various groups within the church. It would also include sales of food at a spaghetti dinner or used goods at a yard sale. Some states have exempted *religious* nonprofit organizations from having to collect sales tax from its customers and remit it to the state. Each state is very different on these requirements.

Sales Tax Refund Request

Many states allow not-for-profit organizations relief from paying sales tax on purchases for their own use when the purchase is made. Others do not share that philosophy. In those states, nongovernmental not-for-profits must pay sales tax on purchases when the purchase is made and must submit a request for reimbursement of these taxes paid.

Conclusion

Perhaps more than any other area, irregularity or scandal in the realm of finances can destroy a congregation or a pastor's ministry. But these simple systems, which are easy to implement, can create an environment of transparency and safety for financial procedures. Observing due diligence with church finances is not difficult or complicated, but it is vital.

8

United Methodist
Denominational Concerns

This chapter addresses reports and concerns particularly for United Methodists.

Preparing for Charge Conference

My first charge conference was on a September Sunday afternoon in 1979. I was serving a part-time student appointment during my senior year of college. I remember it pretty well because it was a disaster. I had been told that there were a lot of forms to fill out and that I had better not wait until the last minute to get started. Thinking I was being radically proactive, I began preparing the Friday before the charge conference. All I can say is the district superintendent and the laity (except one) were very kind.

Now I know that preparations for charge conference begin in midsummer. Often pastors will receive their apportionments and their charge conference date in July. This is important, because it takes about two or three months to prepare for it. At this meeting, either the district superintendent (D.S.) or another elder appointed by the D.S. will preside. The pastor's salary will be set, reports will be received from committees such as finance and trustees, and officers for the coming year will be elected.

Most pastors have more contact with their superintendent during this meeting than during the rest of the year put together. It is your big opportunity to demonstrate to the D.S. that you are a good pastor, leader, and administrator. Shine, by being meticulously prepared and by helping your people share the uplifting story of their ministry. Praise your people to the D.S.; see that light shines upon the beautiful and faithful aspects of their ministry. The D.S. will know that if the ministry of the laity is inspiring and effective, then the ministry of the pastor must be too. This will also gratify your lay leadership. Do everything you can to ensure that snags are worked out well before the day of charge conference. If you foresee an impending problem that cannot be sorted out, give the D.S. advance warning. If you are in doubt about how anything should be prepared for charge conference, call the district office; they will be glad to give you all the help you need to succeed.

In preparation for charge conference, the staff-parish relations committee (SPRC) must meet to recommend the pastor's compensation package for the coming year. The package includes salary, travel, utilities, continuing education funds, acceptance of the insurance and pension amounts, and if a parsonage is not provided, an adequate housing allowance. This meeting will need to be held early enough so that the salary recommendation can be presented to the finance committee and the church council before going to the charge conference. It is traditional in many churches for the minister to be excused while the committee deliberates his salary; however, the *Discipline* gives the pastor the right to stay for the deliberations if he chooses. I usually let the SPRC chair know politely, before the meeting starts, that I will remain for the entire meeting. The *Discipline* gives us that privilege for a reason. The same is true for the meeting when the pastor is evaluated. People's private opinions are important, but they are not as important as their public decisions. I want to be there when the public decisions that profoundly affect me and my family are debated.

The pastor should also call a meeting of the committee on lay leadership. Nominations will be made for officers whose terms have expired, or who otherwise must be replaced. There are two ways of doing this. One way is to simply make a list of the offices that need to be filled, call the meeting, and let people brainstorm. This is usually pretty inefficient. There will almost always be a few people on the committee who are in a hurry to get the job done and get home. These folks may be more interested in getting names in slots than in discerning the best leadership choices. The first name suggested usually becomes the nominee. Perhaps a better way is for the pastor to make a list of offices that must be filled and begin talking with trusted people in the congregation (some of whom would be on the committee) about who might be good in those positions. By the time the committee meets, the pastor and several other people at that meeting already know whom they will nominate for key positions. This is good, proactive leadership. If a committee member does not agree with a name suggested for leadership, they can suggest alternatives and the matter can be put to a vote. It is preferable to have a few uncomfortable moments of suggesting alternative nominees than to spend the next three years working with inappropriate leaders. Be especially careful of who is nominated for the committee on lay leadership: they are the rudder that will steer the congregation's boat for years to come.

The pastor may sometimes be accused of "stacking" the nominations with officers she can best work with. While it is genuinely important to have different groups and factions represented in the church leadership, the pastor needs to have leaders in place who share the same vision. The pastor who does not endeavor to place the best persons available in leadership is failing in her responsibility to lead. Were it not the intention of the larger church for the pastor to play a significant role in the selection of officers, the pastor would not have been placed as chair of the committee on lay leadership. Usually, people who accuse the pastor of "stacking" are attempting to disrupt or terminate the pastor's ministry. Since they are unlikely to be placated or pleased, you may as well decide whether you are going to lead or leave. If you intend to lead, then do so, and ignore the whiners who accuse you of stacking.

After new officers are nominated, they must be contacted to see if they will serve. Ordinarily this duty is divided among members of the committee, with each person agreeing to contact those with whom he feels he has the most rapport. About one week later, the committee meets again to see how many openings remain. New persons are nominated and contacted until all openings are filled.

There will often be one or two persons who will forget they agreed to serve; and in January, when they see their name published, will chastise the minister for having presumed upon them. It is a good idea to instruct each member of the nominating committee to have the person they contact sign two copies of a form, within a week of agreeing to serve. This form gives the title of the position(s), along with the beginning and ending dates of service, and has a dated signature line. They give the person one copy and give you the other copy to file.

Similarly, if someone tells you they would like to resign their position before their term expires, it is wise to have them write or e-mail this information to you, so you can file it for future reference. It is not unheard of for someone to say they want to resign, then get confused later and say the pastor replaced them without asking.

Before beginning the nominations process, it is a good idea to refresh oneself on the *Discipline's* requirements for each committee. For example, must members of each committee be professing members of the church? Is there a requirement to have a young adult or youth member of a committee? If you don't want to look it up for yourself, you could always ask your D.S., or call InfoServe (800-251-8140), or contact me at my website (www.johntyson.info). InfoServe is a terrific service. If you have a question about any technical matter concerning United Methodism, the consultants at InfoServe will usually find the answer in short order. If the above number is no longer working, call your conference office and ask for the current number.

In preparation for charge conference, the "Annual Report of the Trustees" will also need to be filled out. It is useful to have last year's report in your hands as you do this, because a lot of the information will be the same. But look at this report in time to allow the trustees to update any information such as insurance coverage, value of church property, or financial holdings.

The "Annual Report of the Committee on Finance" will also need to be filled out. Last year's form will be helpful to you; many of the answers will be the same. Go over it with the finance chair. As soon as the pastor receives notification of the apportionments, this information is shared with the finance chair. At the same finance committee and church council meeting that deals with the SPRC's recommendation for pastoral support, the apportionments should be presented (they are apportioned, and not debatable, although GCFA [General Council on Finance and Administration] may be petitioned for an adjustment). A "Fund Balance Report" form will also have to be filled out, usually at the end of the year.

The pastor will have to prepare the "Report of the Pastor." There is a section where the pastor gives an account of his ministry. Some pastors proudly include the number of visits they have made, but this always raises the question of what, exactly, constitutes a visit. The answers are usually decidedly unedifying (phone calls, impromptu chats in grocery stores, and so on) so this information may be well omitted. It might be more inspiring to speak of leadership endeavors, lay leadership training, and studies taught. You will also have to list the names of people who have been baptized, who have been added to the church rolls, and who have been removed from membership. If people are joining, you will need to note whether they have come from another UMC, other denominations, or whether they are new believers coming by profession of faith. If they are being removed from church rolls, you will need to note the reason, such as transfer to another UMC, to another denomination, withdrawal, charge conference action, or death. This same list will come in handy when you fill out your Table 1 reports; you just have to update it so that it is accurate through the end of the year.

The form called "Minutes of the Charge Conference" will also be required. You can get it and the other forms well ahead of time by ordering them from Cokesbury. If you have questions about any of these forms or the procedures for charge conference, your D.S. or her secretary will be glad to answer the questions for you.

Tables I, II, and III

Tables I, II, and III are forms the pastor is required by General Conference to submit. They are due at the beginning of the year to report on the year that just ended. It is a good idea to look at last year's forms early so you can see what kind of information will be required. Fill them out to the best of your ability.

Table I deals with membership, participation, and assets. To fill out this form, you will need a list of everyone who either joined your congregation, or was taken off your membership roll. You will also need to indicate how they were removed (other denomination, death, withdrawal, and so on) or how they joined (profession of faith, transfer of membership, and so on). This is not difficult information to get, because you, or the membership secretary, recorded it each time someone either joined the church or was removed from the roll. You probably also filed a copy of each newsletter and of each bulletin (we punch holes in ours and keep them in a loose-leaf binder marked with the corresponding year), and these would contain announcements of any membership changes you might have forgotten to record.

You will also be asked to record the average worship attendance at the principle service of worship. This means you will need to have your ushers count the worshipers each Sunday and get that information to you or perhaps to the church secretary. If you have three Sunday morning worship services, include the average of all three.

Table I is also going to ask for the attendance at every spiritual formation group you had last year, including Bible studies, Sunday school, small groups, and Volunteers in Mission (VIM) groups; so either keep a record or prepare to estimate (records are better). This is also where you will record membership in UMW, UMM, and UMYF along with the amounts spent for certain projects. The president and the treasurer of each group will have this information.

Table I is also the place to record information concerning the value of property and assets owned by the church. Most of this information can be found in the trustees report you filed at charge conference.

Table II is usually pretty easy for the pastor because your treasurer or bookkeeper will have all the information that is asked for, such as apportionments and benevolences paid. The amounts apportioned are in your charge conference records with the minutes. If you have a new treasurer or bookkeeper, it is a good idea to make sure they know as soon as they take office what will be expected when it is time to file Table II. It helps to go over a copy of last year's with them if they are new. Since all the General Conference and annual conference mandated special offerings will be reported on their own lines, it is good to remember to take the offerings. If you forget one, it will be obvious when you fill out Table II. The treasurer or bookkeeper will also need to add up everything that was spent on programming, staff, and operating expenses and report these. Table II is particularly important because the information reported there forms the basis for computing your apportionments.

The information required for Table III will be found by consulting the treasurer or bookkeeper and the finance chair because this form essentially traces the origins of monies given. Looking at Table III in advance will ensure these persons are prepared with the necessary answers, such as the number of giving units, amounts received through pledges, through nonpledged gifts, and through offerings that were given in cash with no named contributor. You are also asked to list money raised through sale of church assets, rentals, and fund-raisers. If you have had a capital campaign, you will be asked to list details of contributions. You will also list amounts received for memorials and special gifts. Table III makes it obvious that churches that do not give their membership a challenge and an opportunity to pledge annual financial support are out of step.

Multiple Church Charges

In some ways, multiple point charges are more difficult than "station" churches; in other ways they are easier. They are more difficult because much of the administrative paperwork is multiplied by the number of churches on the charge. For example, Tables I, II, and III have to be filled out for each church. So do all of the charge conference forms. The smaller the church the less likely it is that the treasurer is going to be quasi-professional, so the pastor will probably have more detailed work to do when it is time to fill out these reports. There may also be more meetings to attend, because each church must have its own meetings of SPRC, trustees, church council, and so on. Joint charge meetings may be held in addition to the individual church meetings, and you will probably have a far larger geographical area to cover for these meetings and pastoral care, so driving time and expenses may be greater than at a station church.

On the other hand, there are some advantages. At multiple point charges, the expectations of the pastor tend to be pretty simple: preach, give basic administrative structure, and visit. There is usually less demand for office hours, because there typically is not a centralized church office. Since the pastor is dividing her time among several churches, there is less effort to control how the pastor spends her time. And there is often at least one church where things feel positive, even if other churches on the charge feel less so. It is nice to have a haven like that. Each of the small churches tend to have a matriarch or patriarch. If the pastor will consult frequently with this person, and give them sway, the rest of leading this congregation will take care of itself. It is entirely pointless for you to get into a significant disagreement with this person; ultimately, they will prevail.

How the pastor administrates each church depends on the size of the church. I have pastored two churches with an average attendance of twelve people; it is nonsense to attempt a lot of different administrative meetings in a church of this size. It is useful to ask the people, the previous pastor, or the D.S., how things have been done in the past and use that as your pattern. Very small churches tend to have administrative meetings that deal with all the church's business at once, because the same six people are on all the committees. It is also convenient that a lot of things tend to get settled either before or after worship, because everyone present is a member of the church council. This means that often, you don't have to go to separate meetings to attend to the church's business. But at larger churches on the charge individual meetings will have to be scheduled.

Most churches on charges like to maintain their individuality, and it is not unusual to have internecine disagreements and jealousies. For these reasons joint ministries are usually difficult to promote, but they are nevertheless a wise strategy. Bible studies, youth ministries, men's ministries, and mission projects are good subjects for joint effort. Gathering a few people from each congregation can give you a group large enough to accomplish something. And even though you may have no one from the other churches go to your Bible study held at Ebenezer Church, if you present it as a joint study it may prevent you from having to teach three Bible studies, in three different communities, on three different nights, with three people present. By having joint projects, the onus is placed on the people to take advantage of the ministry opportunities you provide, and there is the prospect of greater impact when you join forces with other churches on your charge.

Perhaps the greatest pastoral contribution you can make to each church is to help them discover and address just one felt need of their community. If you can help them focus their outreach on one such ministry, it might help them to rediscover their relevance to the community. This could provide a center of significance and identity for the tiny congregation. It could be a turning point.

Most of the privileges and responsibilities of the churches on a charge are in proportion to the amount of salary they provide. Usually, all these things are worked out when the charge is established and the pattern for worship services is set up. If one church owns the parsonage, the other churches pay some sort of compensation, usually in proportion to what they pay of the salary.

The trustees of the church that owns the parsonage are usually responsible for the house itself, while the charge typically shares responsibility for furnishing the parsonage. There is usually a charge parsonage committee. If two or more churches share ownership of the parsonage, the percentage of ownership is usually specified in the deed.

Each charge has one member of annual conference. Frequently, the churches will rotate this responsibility, but it also has much to do with who can go. Each church has its own SPRC, but there may also be a charge SPRC. This is the one that does pastoral evaluations and is consulted about the appointment of pastors. There may also be a board of trustees for the charge and a committee on lay leadership for the charge. If there are such committees, all churches on the charge must be represented. Usually, the proportion of membership is proportional to the salary each church pays. There must be a charge treasurer to handle the pastor's salary and pension, because only one check for the pastor's pension and insurance can be written; this check cannot be written by the preacher. Most churches pay salary individually, but the conference and the General Board of Pensions will only take one check per charge.

Conclusion

If you know in advance what information will be required for charge conference and your year-end reports, you will be fore-armed. Coupled with the timeline for nominations and budgeting, you will have plenty of tools in place to prepare for these denominational responsibilities. Your D.S. will always be glad to answer any questions about this process and so will your fellow pastors. The same holds true for questions concerning your multi-church charge. Most of the patterns for administrative processes in multi-church charges are put in place by the D.S. when the charge is set up. When in doubt, don't hesitate to ask. And if you feel like it, you are always welcome to give me a shout through my website (www.johntyson.info).